D0572441

F

REBA McENTIRE

THE QUEEN OF COUNTRY

CAROL LEGGETT

A FIRESIDE BOOK
Published by Simon & Schuster
New York London Toronto Sydney Tokyo Singapore

FIRESIDE
Simon & Schuster Building
Rockefeller Center
1230 Avenue of the Americas
New York, New York 10020

Manufactured in the United States of America

1 3 5 7 9 10 8 6 4 2

Library of Congress Cataloging-in-Publication Data
is available.

ISBN 0-671-75141-7

CONTENTS

STARTING OVER

Monday, March 25, 1991. In the Dorothy Chandler Pavilion, the sixty-third annual Academy Awards were in full swing. The crowded hall was jammed with the most glamorous celebrities, including Madonna and Michael Jackson, who were seated in the front row. Bored stars milled around, their "replacements"—good-looking young men and women in evening wear—sitting in the seats so the TV audience wouldn't feel cheated.

There was a murmur around the hall that Reba McEntire was about to appear. Everybody sat down, stopped talking, and turned rapt attention to the stage. The lights dimmed. The orchestra began to play the first notes of "I'm Checkin' Out," the Oscar-nominated song from Carrie Fisher's *Postcards from the Edge,* starring Meryl Streep, Dennis Quaid, and Shirley MacLaine. An almost eerie hush fell over the audience as Reba, the "Queen of Country," emerged, swathed in green sequins, launching into her plaintive-edged performance.

Alone on the huge stage (in contrast to the other performers, who had been accompanied by singers, dancers, and special-effects galore) with her fiery red hair, blue saucer eyes, 50,000-watt voice, and a twang that can "bend guitar strings and break hearts," Reba McEntire's deep emotional pain was laid bare to the millions of people around the world who watched. As the camera zoomed in for a close-up, her eyes brimmed over with tears. Even for the jaded Hollywood crowd, it was a deeply affecting moment. The minute the song ended, they jumped to their feet in a frenzy, and gave Reba their outpouring of love and sympathy with a standing ovation that seemed to go on forever. The hardworking, Okie cowgirl-turned-superstar was clearly overwhelmed.

Nine days earlier, Reba McEntire had lost almost her entire band in a fiery plane crash. Devastated and in seclusion (except for a March 20 memorial service), Reba, who described "pain so great it made me numb inside—I barely knew I was alive," made the decision to appear at the Academy Awards. "I did this for my band. They're checking out. They've got a new place to dwell."

The appearance was Reba's tribute to her lost friends, but she also found it an ordeal to show her pain so publicly. Afterward, Reba and her husband, Narvel, went home to work through their grief. A saddened McEntire mused about her future: "It'll never be the same without my family. I'll have a new family and I'll accept and love them. But those people [the eight who died in the crash] will be very special in my heart forever."

1 RIDING, RANCHING, AND THE RODEO

The original roots of the McEntire clan can be traced back to the shores of Scotland and Ireland. However, Reba's grandfather, John McEntire, was born in Indian country—Lula, Oklahoma. Family legend has it that Grandfather McEntire's "folks" were boisterous, colorful, larger-than-life characters who had moved to Oklahoma from Texas—their reasons for leaving being the stuff of speculation and western legend. The McEntires apparently had started out as ranchers; John was the first in the family to work in the rodeo. He joined the Wild West Show when it came through town, then traveled with it all over the country. In many ways, being on the road gave the McEntire men—great achievers by nature—a sense of the world beyond the state lines of Oklahoma, an evolving sophistication and stature they shared with their families.

John McEntire gradually mastered the various rodeo skills, although it was at roping that he made a name for himself. After saving up enough cash to get a piece of land and several head of cattle, he became a rancher; because of the hard financial times—this was during the 1930s and the Depression—he still had to work the rodeo to make enough money. Fortunately, his wife, Alice, was a well-educated school teacher—rare at that time in rural Oklahoma or anywhere else. (In fact, teaching was something of a tradition among the McEntire women, and even Reba was at one time headed toward a career as a teacher.)

Reba's father, Clark McEntire, followed his father's lead by working the rodeo as well. He started steer-roping on the rodeo circuit at the age of twelve, winning his first world championship title at age sixteen. He saved the money he made from the competitions, even though rodeo circuit life was expensive to maintain—there were lots of costs for the competitors. John wisely invested his

Clark McEntire takes control at the 1963 National Rodeo Finals in Rawhuska, Oklahoma.

Courtesy of the Professional Rodeo Cowboys Association

Clark McEntire, Reba's father, became a rodeo champion while still in his teens.

earnings in a big cattle ranch in nearby Chockie (near the Chockie Mountains) that would provide security for himself, and for a family when they came along. Clark had grown up in nearby Kiowa, a rural, very flat, and not terribly prosperous part of Oklahoma. It was there, however, that Clark met and fell in love with Jacqueline Smith.

Jacqueline, called Jackie, was blessed with a beautiful voice many compared to the late Patsy Cline (one of Reba's musical idols—"I read everything I can get on her—nobody yet has sung better"), but she never pursued a singing career, though she wanted to. The times didn't allow it. Besides, her parents were Baptists and very religious; they frowned on the idea of a virtuous young woman getting into "entertainment." Instead, Jackie went to college, got a teaching degree, and later was too busy with her family even to consider singing professionally.

Clark McEntire and Jackie were married in Atoka, Oklahoma, in March of 1950. The simple ceremony was held at the local Baptist church. Their first child, Alice Lynn, was born in December of 1951. A son, Dale (who became known as Pake for Pecos Pete—a family nickname), came along a year and a half later. Reba was born almost two years later, and the youngest of the four McEntire kids, Martha Susan (Susie), was born in November 1957.

When Reba Nell McEntire was born on March 28, 1955, it was the era of "I Like Ike," a conservative time in which traditional family values were prized, as personified on TV by the Cleavers on "Leave It to Beaver" and the almost too-perfect Nelson family depicted on "Ozzie and Harriet."

It was a time of national fascination with cowboys and with the image of the rugged individualist with simple goals and an overriding sense of decency. These interests were also reflected in television shows like "Davey Crockett" and "Rawhide." Even the popular children's show "The Mickey Mouse Club" featured episodes of "Spin and Marty" depicting neophyte cowboys. Buffalo Bob was the puppet master of everybody's favorite jeans- and bandana-clad partner, Howdy Doody. Roy Rogers, Dale Evans, and Trigger were welcome guests in living rooms all across the country.

Despite all the interest in cowboys and simple values, however, country music, which got its start as mountain music in the Appalachians, remained limited in its appeal, was still considered primarily the voice of rural America. Its songs, with lyrics that told of lost love, that celebrated the joys of family closeness, that emphasized love of God and country, were drowned out by the rapidly emerging sound of rock and roll and the phenomenon of pop celebrity. Even so, it had its stars. Miss Kitty Wells, known as the Grand Dame of Country, was on the charts in 1955 (the year Reba McEntire was born)—the only woman ever accorded that honor.

Certainly at that time, the biggest name in music of any kind was the "King of Rock and Roll," Elvis Presley, who burst onto the scene with a whole new way of singing and a whole new style of music. His sound, a blend of country and "race music," set the music world on fire, with a profound and lasting effect on generations to come. Country singers like Patsy Cline and Kitty Wells may have laid the groundwork for the career Reba McEntire eventually would enjoy, but it was Presley who redefined celebrity and, in the process, set the standards by which all others would be judged.

Even though she's reached the pinnacle of success, McEntire still thinks of herself as "just plain Reba."

THE EARLY YEARS 2

By now, the story of how Reba Nell McEntire made it into the country music business is as familiar to her fans as Loretta Lynn's story of struggle and success told in *The Coalminer's Daughter*. But, like any good tale, it bears repeating.

Life in the McEntire family perhaps was not always easy, but it was often fun, filled with colorful experiences. Certainly everybody anywhere near McAlester, Oklahoma, where Reba was born, knew who the McEntires were. Clark was a famous rodeo champion, and there were lots of family members in the area to spread stories of his successes. And while there was never a surplus of money, there was always adventure. In the summer months, Clark took his family along with him on the rodeo circuit. In the winter everybody got involved with ranching at the family spread. It was fun but sometimes chaotic for the youngsters to go from the fast-paced, crowd-filled world of the rodeo back to the ranch, "out in the middle of nowhere." Because of the isolation of rural life, where there was virtually nothing to do in the way of entertainment because of the strong influence of the Baptist church, family was all-important.

Clark taught Pake the skills he needed to compete in the rodeo, and he taught Reba as well how to rope and to ride the barrel races. In time, Reba got very good at it, and competed all over the Southwest, winning many contests. Jackie, frustrated in her own desire for some kind of career in music, taught her kids to sing. On the long, overnight drives to rodeos in exotic-sounding places like Cheyenne and Thermopolis, throughout the states of Wyoming, Colorado, Oregon, Texas, and Montana, the McEntires would all cram into their old green Ford. It was far from glamorous, but it was fun, a family, close together for hours. Reba fondly recalls those good old days, with all the kids wedged into the backseat: "Susie and I would sleep on the floorboard, Alice would get the seat, and Pake wedged himself in behind the seat."

Pake McEntire in a roping competition, Denver 1976.

Courtesy of the Professional Rodeo Cowboys Association

These car trips could get tedious, of course, and the kids did get restless and bored, so they'd wrestle and pinch each other, making lots of noise that tested their father's patience. "There was no radio in the car, so Mama would teach us to sing harmony to entertain us," Reba recalls. All that beautiful music served another purpose, too—it kept Clark McEntire wide awake and alert for the drive. The songs they chose were usually amusing little ditties like "Wake Up, Little Susie" or "Please, Mr. Custer." Sometimes, however, the McEntires, all raised as Baptists, would sing gospel hymns from church.

It became apparent, even at an early age, that Reba possessed a golden singing voice. Her family was impressed, especially by her mastery of harmony, which is the backbone of country music.

All the McEntires agree that Reba Nell was the most spoiled member of the family. Alice was fond of saying, "Whatever Little Reba wants, Little Reba gets!" Plus she was a ham, making herself the center of attention whenever possible.

Reba's first big break in "show biz" came at the age of five. The McEntires had arrived in Cheyenne for Frontier Days, the most important of all rodeo events and the setting for a much-told tale in Reba-lore. The whole family was packed into a single room in the Cheyenne Hotel, and since there was no television in their room, they hung around the lobby, looking for something fun to do. Pake told Reba that he had just earned some money for entertaining a group of rodeo guys with his version of an Elvis song, "Hound Dog." She wanted to make some money, too, so she begged Pake to sing a couple of songs with her. The two launched into "Jesus Loves Me," and somebody gave Reba a

"Coming in at night, it would be so dark that all you could see were the sparks from the horses' shoes hitting the rocks. We'd sing just to keep ourselves awake."

nickel for her performance. "I was amazed, even though I earned it," said the fledgling superstar. "After that, I was hooked!"

The next year, Reba "debuted" in a starring role in her first-grade Christmas pageant at the Kiowa School, singing "Away in the Manger." "From grade school through college, I was in every musical program I could get into," she remembers. And from the very beginning, her ambitions were supported by both her parents: "Mama and Daddy always inspired me to sing. I'd be out tryin' to run barrels or haul hay, and Daddy (who was so proud of my talent) would tell me to get in the house and practice my music. So, I'd spend endless hours at the piano, or strumming my guitar, singing my favorite songs."

Ranching, too, provided frequent opportunity for the McEntire kids to sing together. The entire operation was a family affair; everybody got involved in herding cattle on the 8,000-acre spread. Reba, a wild tomboy who was always "doing her own thing," always looking for a little excitement, paints an evocative picture of her daily life as a child: "We'd get up before the sun, eat breakfast, and ride out on horses, trying to get the cattle back toward the house. Coming in at night, it would be so dark that all you could see were the sparks from the horses' shoes hitting the rocks. We'd sing just to keep ourselves awake."

As Reba went into junior high, Richard Nixon was elected President of the United States and the war in Vietnam was growing more and more costly. These things had little impact on her life, however. Oklahoma remained the same, seemingly impervious to the changes taking place elsewhere. Lots of things that city folks took for granted, like shopping centers, fast food outlets, and lots of things to do, were missing from the McEntires' corner of the world. Their's remained a quiet, rural existence, still very much influenced by the strictures and dictates of the Baptist church. For Reba, who was always popular and always on the lookout for fun, the most excitement came either from the local 4-H club (a popular pastime in rural communities) or from sports—she excelled in basketball.

All her years of harmonizing with her brother and sister Susie ("Alice never sang much") paid off—they formed the Singing McEntires. The trio performed all over the rodeo circuit, singing whenever they weren't competing. When they weren't out with the rodeo, they earned as much as $13 a

Courtesy of the Professional Rodeo Cowboys Association

Susie, Pake, and Reba—the Singing McEntires. "Sometimes we'd play for $13 a night!"

night putting on shows in neighboring towns. It was a promising beginning. (Pake went on to his own singing and songwriting career; sister Susie sings gospel music with her husband, Paul, a minister in Oklahoma.)

Clark Rhyne, a teacher at Kiowa High School in the '60s and now principal of that school, was an old friend of the McEntires. As is typical in such close-knit communities, their families were even related by marriage a few generations back. Jackie McEntire, who had helped her children write, record, and even press a song about John McEntire, wanted an organized musical program for all the local kids. To this end, she convinced Rhyne to help out with a school marching band. Not surprisingly, they called it the Kiowa Cowboy Band; what they played was completely predictable—country music! The band played at 4-H dances, football games, even country fairs, winning a passel of talent competitions. Reba, singing alone, won a contest that awarded her a car for six months.

At some point, Clark Rhyne, his wife, and baby chaperoned a trip Reba and some of her classmates took to Pike's Peak. One of Rhyne's proudest possessions is a photograph of him and Reba at the mountain's top. Says Rhyne, "We always figured that Reba would get somewhere with all that talent, but if we'd known how famous she was going to be, we'd have taken lots more pictures of her!"

During the late '60s, rock and roll had become unquestionably the dominant style of music. The raw sound of rock's earliest days had been succeeded by the Motown sound, which in turn was followed by the Beatles and the whole British Invasion. By the time Reba graduated from high school, the psychedelic sounds that had flowered in San Francisco had been replaced by the disco sounds of groups like the Bee Gees.

Reba's boyfriend in high school was a hardcore rock fan and tried his best to get her interested in it. While she had an appreciation for just about any kind of music, Reba remained a staunch country music fan, having inherited her mother's love of Patsy Cline. She was also inspired by country stars like Dolly Parton, Loretta Lynn, and Anne Murray (all of whom became close friends years later), and loved the subtle pop tunes of Barbra Streisand.

During the '60s, and continuing into the '70s, while in many quarters of the world young people were rebelling against the establishment, protesting the Vietnam war, and announcing "God is dead," Reba continued to embrace her religion and traditional ideals. Country folk, perhaps by virtue of the fact they were cut off from the mainstream, were more conservative. They were staunchly proud of their family and cultural heritage, and were not shy in letting the rest of the world know how they felt. This sentiment was given voice most clearly in the Merle Haggard song "I'm an Okie from Muskogee," which gained national attention in the early 1970s.

Throughout this turbulent era the McEntires remained steadfast in their religious faith, attending the local Baptist church every Sunday. This early religious training continues to influence Reba, who contends she could not have pursued her singing career without her faith and the support she feels from God. To this day, when times are tough, she turns to him for guidance and the patience to cope.

"I thank the Lord every day for all that he has done for me," she says. "When I want to get straight with him, I pray a bunch. God has my future planned, so I don't have to worry about what will happen."

Church is also where Reba got her love of gospel tunes, a few of which show up in her stage show from time to time. "Somebody Up There Likes Me" was included on her gold-selling *Live* album, and "I Know I'll Have a Better Day Tomorrow" was one of her early recordings. Reba has said that someday she hopes to record a whole album of gospel music.

3 NASHVILLE'S IDENTITY CRISIS

Country and western, one of the few forms of truly indigenous American music, was born as bluegrass up in the hills of Virginia and Kentucky. The settlers there were of generally English ancestry, with some Scottish and Irish names mixed in. These pioneers had brought with them the music drawn from the tradition of English balladeers. Without much in the way of material goods, and isolated from the rest of the world, these "hillbillies," as they were called, would get together for sing-alongs, accompanying their tunes with banjos, dobros, fiddles, guitars, and occasionally even the family washboard. This musical genre evolved, spreading westward and centering eventually in Nashville, which became the capital of country music radio and the home of the Grand Ole Opry.

When Elvis Presley appeared on the music scene, he was heralded as the creator of a brand-new sound. In fact, Elvis came squarely out of the country music tradition, which in turn heavily influenced rock. He started out on "The Louisiana Hayride," a radio show that featured country greats like Johnny Horton and Hank Snow. But in those days there were very few country radio stations and little chance for country singers to reach the kind of mass audience that was available to pop stars. While country music "purists" like Hank Williams, Sr., and Webb Pierce stuck to their guns and their traditional style of singing, other singers emerged in the '50s and '60s—country-based singers like Elvis, Carl Perkins, and Johnny Cash—who were able to skyrocket to fame and fortune by combining musical styles. Country sounds mixed with "race" music (r & b) allowed them to "cross over" to a new, popular hybrid that won them more air play and reached a much greater number of fans. Presley, adding to the music his own brand of magic and sexy charisma, elevated his personal sound into an art form that proved to be a major catalyst for contemporary rock and roll, and has continued to influence music-makers for decades. Today, people tend to forget that country music was both the origin and the major artistic influence on these new superstars, so greatly did they overshadow their contemporaries who stuck with a pure country sound.

Eventually, however, everybody in Nashville wanted a piece of crossover fame. The formula that emerged from this frenzy, "the Nashville Sound," turned out to be somewhat sterile. Often ill-produced, the result was a bland combination of country and pop that had little appeal to either camp. Despite its lack of relative commercial success, however, Nashville pushed on with "the Nashville

Sound," hoping it would eventually catch on in a big way.

Until the '70s, Nashville was hardly a major force in the music business. Two or three of the major record labels had branch offices there, but only a few recording studios were available, and there was a limited supply of session musicians. According to Jimmy Bowen, a major figure in country music and currently the president of Capitol (Records) Nashville, the problem was "there were a dozen guys playing the same old track—only the lead singer changed." Bowen, who came out of Los Angeles and a solid pop/rock background, was president of MGM Records in L.A. during the mid-'70s. He first came to Nashville to check out the record company's small country division. "What I saw was a town in a real embryonic stage, but I had the feeling that something big was going to come out of here—that this place had huge commercial potential."

Jimmy Bowen soon relocated to Nashville, followed in due time by a flock of other L.A.- and New York–based music biz types. Then the talent, singers and musicians, started to travel to Nashville as well. Things started to change, although crossover was still the name of the game. Hank Williams, Jr., country royalty with rock leanings despite his big ten-gallon hat, sold a million records (he was produced by Bowen). The movie *Urban Cowboy,* starring John Travolta and Debra Winger, suddenly made it hip to play at being a cowboy, and the movie featured a strong country-oriented music score.

The mainstream pop scene was getting stale, so country was the new "flavor of the week." The list of success stories got longer—Dolly Parton, Mickey Gilley, Eddie Rabbitt, Barbara Mandrell, Kenny Rogers—their records were selling like hotcakes; they got TV shows, even movie deals. Nashville was proving that it was possible to make big-time money with country music, that there was a brand-new mass market for this old and familiar sound. Smelling large profits, every major record company began establishing a presence in Nashville.

Then, of course, the furor died down. The fickle public cooled its passion for country; nobody wanted to be a cowboy anymore. All this flux meant that crossover mania got even stronger, with money as the strong, enduring incentive. "What we wound up with," says Bowen, "was a bunch of crap. It was a diluted, slick-sounding mess that was trying to be something it wasn't."

Such was the music world Reba McEntire walked into when she began her career in Nashville in 1974.

4 REBA GOES TO NASHVILLE

After graduation from high school, Reba, like her mother before her, went off to college. She attended Southeastern Oklahoma State in Durant, majoring in elementary education and planning to be a teacher (like Jackie) when she graduated. Reba's minor was music. In particular, she studied classical piano, Mozart, and theory—training that Reba acknowledged "sure didn't hurt" her singing and songwriting skills years later.

In 1974, Reba's whole life changed. That summer, Clark McEntire suggested she try to get a job at the National Rodeo Finals, since she'd be hanging around anyway. He introduced her to a friend of his, and Reba won the chance to sing the National Anthem (she's been known to call it her favorite song) at the event. She'd even get to be on national TV—a huge thrill—as the rodeo was being covered by ABC's "Wide World of Sports."

The man who would "discover" Reba McEntire heard her sing the National Anthem that day. Red

For the demo, Reba sang four songs, including one she had composed herself, "Leave My Texas Boy Alone." Then it was back to school.

Steagall, a native Texan, had a song on the country charts at the time, "Someone Cares for You"—one of many hits in his recording career. A former music publishing partner of Jimmy Bowen's in Los Angeles, Steagall was impressed by Reba's performance that day, though her style was nothing like it is today. "She was trying awfully hard to sing like Barbra Streisand," recalls Red.

Later that day, at a rodeo party in the hospitality suite of a local hotel, Reba sang another tune, accompanying herself on guitar. Jackie approached Red Steagall and asked him if he could help get the Singing McEntires signed to a record deal in Nashville. Jackie, who has always said she lives vicariously through her talented daughter, dreamed of a singing career for Reba. "Red turned me down," recalls Mrs. McEntire. "He was concentrating on his own career, and barely keeping his head above water."

By next January, however, Steagall had called Chockie Mountain, agreeing to make a demo with Reba, whose beautiful and powerful voice had stuck in his mind.

Reba was away in college when the call came from Steagall, but during that semester's spring break, Jackie drove her daughter to Nashville. The family had vacationed there previously, stopping in to see a performance at the legendary Grand Ole Opry. For the demo, Reba sang four songs, including one she had composed herself, "Leave My Texas Boy Alone." Then it was back to school.

Red explained to Reba that it was going to take some time to shop her demo around, and advised her to go back to her normal, everyday life, which she did.

In the meantime, another life-altering experi-

Courtesy of the Country Music Foundation, Inc.

A fresh-faced girl from Oklahoma makes it big in Nashville.

ence took place. Again, it was in a familiar setting—at the rodeo.

During the summer of 1975 in Lubbock, Texas, Reba, just barely out of her teens, was introduced to a friend of Pake's, champion steer-wrestler Charlie Battles—who was thirty-one at the time. Feeling shy and unsure of herself, Reba convinced herself that the dark, muscular Charlie was interested in her sister Alice. But they kept bumping into each other on the rodeo circuit all summer, and before long Reba and Charlie were smitten with each other. Charlie had been married in 1966 but was now divorced; he had two preteen sons, Lance and Cody. By the end of the year, Charlie Battles and Reba McEntire were engaged.

Nineteen seventy-five proved to be a year of great new beginnings for Reba, busy as she was with college classes and a new romance. Red Steagall called: "Come back down to Nashville; I think we've got a bite!"

Reba, in her usual modest way, attributes her contract with Mercury Records to just the luck of the draw: "Red took my tape over to Polygram/Mercury. A producer there, who had my tape and another girl's, was told that the company had room for one female singer and he could put anyone on that he wanted—and it was me."

Some fifteen months after her first meeting with Red, on November 11, Reba signed the recording contract with Mercury. An optimist by nature, and coming from a family of winners, she was confident that she would not only survive in the record biz, but make it all the way to the top in style!

Early in the new year, she recorded four songs picked by producer Glenn Keener—"I Don't Want to Be a One Night Stand," "I'm Not Your Kind of Girl," "A Boy Like You," and "I'll Give It to You."

Almost immediately, Reba's voice was recognized as something phenomenal. Her cowgirl twang, with its three-octave range—"almost operatic in its emotional force and precision," as one critic described it—catapulted her into the same class with legends like her own beloved Patsy Cline, Loretta Lynn, Tammy Wynette, and Kitty Wells. The raw emotion and passion she put into her singing, along with eloquent phrasing and vocal acrobatics, seemed to guarantee superstardom to this college coed trying for her first big break.

It was a heady time for the young girl, and Red warned Reba not to be overanxious. He told her to plan on working hard for at least five years before she would start to get the recognition she wanted, and counseled her not to crumble under the pres-

A girlish Reba at the beginning of her fantastic career.

sure and the uncertainty of the crazy music business. Yes, Reba had talent, but a flourishing career would take so much more. As it turned out, it was almost a decade before this Okie cowgirl realized her dreams of superstardom, ten years of struggle before she gained recognition as the undisputed Queen of Country.

The first single, "I Don't Want to Be a One Night Stand," was released during Reba's summer break from school, around the same time she married Charlie Battles. The wedding took place on June 21 at the Baptist church in Stringtown, and by all accounts it was a very traditional ceremony. Instead of going off on a honeymoon like a normal newlywed couple, however, the pair hopped into their camper-pickup and spent the day after the wedding visiting disc jockeys, with Reba trying to promote her newly released record. From the start, it was obvious that McEntire was a tireless workaholic who would devote herself—no holds barred—to becoming a star.

For the next three months, Mr. and Mrs. Battles traveled around the country like nomads. Reba chatted up her record and appeared at small club dates, garnering a small but loyal following. Charlie squeezed in as many rodeo appearances as he could, with his number one fan, Reba, always by his side.

In early September, before going back to college for her final semester, Reba returned to Nashville for another recording session, this time with Jerry Kennedy, who would be her producer throughout her tenure at Mercury. McEntire's voice was so powerful that two limiters (used to prevent instruments from distorting on tape) had to be called into service, when even the use of one is rare.

This time, Reba recorded three songs—"Between a Woman and a Man," "I Was Glad to Give My Everything to You," and "I've Waited All My Life for You." In December, the newly married lady and professional songstress graduated from Southeastern Oklahoma State with a Bachelor's degree. However, her initial objective, a teaching career, was no longer under serious consideration, with Nashville fame beckoning. For the holidays, Reba and Charlie got off the road for a brief respite, settling into their love nest, a primitive house rented to them by Jackie McEntire's boss.

FALSE IDENTITY 5

Reba's first four singles didn't do much—they stayed at the bottom of the country charts and then disappeared. In April 1977, Reba returned to Nashville for two days in the studio, laying down tracks for six more songs. Usually, record companies wouldn't release a full album until a fledgling artist had a bona fide hit, but Mercury felt it was only a matter of time until Reba took off. So late in 1977, they released her first album, called simply *Reba McEntire*.

Nashville, still bonded in an unholy marriage with Los Angeles pop, tried to take the country out of Reba. Her producers tried to refashion her singing into a slick, phoney style that wasn't her—or anybody else, for that matter. The cover of her first LP showed a young, innocent Reba clad in frills, her curly locks draped seductively around her face. She was none too happy with the treatment she was getting, musical and otherwise, but as an inexperienced and often insecure newcomer, chose to keep her mouth closed and do what she was told—at least for the time being.

The *Reba McEntire* album featured three very pop pieces—"Right Time of the Night"; a cover of a Jennifer Warnes (known for her 1980s mega-hit duet with Joe Cocker—"When the Eagle Flies") song, "Glad I Waited Just for You"; and "Angel in Your Arms," originally done by Vivian Bell. "One to One" was a ballad, while the rest of the album dealt with those good old country staples, love and lust—"I Don't Want to Be a One Night Stand," "I've Waited All My Life for You," "I Was Glad to Give My Everything to You," "Take Your Love Away," "Between a Woman and a Man," a Loretta Lynn winner called "Why Can't He Be You?" and a Ray Price oldie, "Invitation to the Blues." There were lots of different styles represented on the album, but very few of them were Oklahoma country—and none of them was the real Reba McEntire.

The album's performance was nothing spectacular, but it helped get Reba's name around, and it garnered her a few more club dates. Then, at the end of 1977, Reba got the thrill of a lifetime: She was invited to perform at the Grand Ole Opry—a real milestone in her fledgling career. Too nervous and shy to introduce herself to the array of luminaries backstage, Reba went on and sang one of the most beautiful songs in the country realm—Patsy Cline's "Sweet Dreams." Singing in a clear, undiluted, almost soprano voice, McEntire stunned the audience, and impressed them with the realization that this was a woman with major talent.

There were lots of different styles represented on the album, but very few of them were Oklahoma country—and none of them was the real Reba McEntire.

Those early days were not easy, however, and the good times were few and far between. Reba was still a relative nobody and occasionally her ego suffered big blows. Since she didn't have her own

"Howdy, y'all!" Reba autographs her very first album at Fan Fair.

band yet, she was forced to sing in front of whoever the opening act was. Sometimes, it would be Red Steagall's band. On other occasions, it would be a rock band that didn't have a clue about any of her songs. There was also a lot of nasty treatment from male stars whose bands didn't want to be bothered.

In 1978 there was a horrible incident in Fort Worth. The only song Reba and the backup band could agree on was "Proud Mary." When that was over, a flustered Reba reverted to some lame joke-telling, and was promptly hooted down. She had to leave the stage. "At times I couldn't draw flies.

A Nashville thrush at one of her earliest performances, forced to sing pop.

Once, I sat in a store to sign autographs, and the only person who came up to me asked where the bathroom was!"

Reba claims she enjoyed those early experiences, despite the occasional unpleasantness. They taught her what she did and didn't want, and the taste of rejection made her even more determined to do things the right way—her way—once she was running the show.

As soon as she could, Reba put her own band together. This move was a step toward taking control, not an easy thing to achieve in the predominantly male and heavily chauvinistic world of Music City. Says Jimmy Bowen, "Country music was run by a bunch of redneck, hillbilly macho men. Their mentality about gal singers was, get ones with big hair, big boobs and short skirts. The producers would tell the women, 'Here's your song, babe. Now sing it and go home.' " Already trying to buck the system, Reba and her hand-picked musicians toured the Southwest, hauling instruments and equipment in a pickup truck and converted horse trailer.

She spent more and more time in Nashville, but was still an outsider, a visitor. Her great strength during this period was, as always, her family. Reba still had dreams that the Singing McEntires would get a record deal.

At a 1978 record biz party, Reba shares a laugh with Mercury executive Charlie Fach (left) and the producer of her first eight albums, Jerry Kennedy (right).

In the meantime, when Susie graduated from school, she acted as Reba's personal assistant at the office in Oklahoma and on the road. But Susie got pregnant and had to stop working. "The smell of diesel fuel [from the bus] started making her sick and she had to go home."

Brother Pake was also a recipient of Reba's generosity. Invited to appear with his sister at some of her club dates as a backup singer, she helped him get a record deal on the Cross label.

Mercury planned to have Reba record an album a year to keep "product" flowing, and released her second album, *Out of a Dream*, in the fall of 1979. It was preceded by three singles (featured on the LP) that briefly appeared on the country charts. *Out of a Dream*'s most popular (and some say best) song was Reba's version of Patsy Cline's "Sweet Dreams." There was also a duet with Jacky Ward, "That Makes Two of Us," and a song Reba wrote on the way home from a rodeo, "Daddy." Two ballads, "Now and Then" and "Rain Fallin'," are sad and lamenting—as ballads are supposed to be—with the remainder of the songs featuring the joys and torments of love: "Last Night Every Night," "Make Me Feel Like a Woman Wants to Feel," "I'm a Woman," "Runaway Heart," and "It's Gotta Be Love."

Reba was getting a few good reviews, most of them identifying her as a gifted up-and-coming singer, but one among many. Sales were far from spectacular, and it was apparent she was not attracting a "big numbers audience." Music critics mostly categorized her in the press as "just another country pop thrush singing bland, watered-down crossover fodder," which is what Nashville was churning out in that era. The powers-that-be had shoved her into making records with overly lush

Reba shows him how to do it—Mercury label mate Jacky Ward (right).

© Alan L. Mayor

Reba gets ready to record a duet with Jacky Ward in 1978—"Three Sheets in the Wind," one of her earliest successes.

© Alan L. Mayor

production values—violins and background choirs that all but obscured her gorgeous voice.

In the image department, Reba, who felt most at home wearing a pair of jeans and her father's rodeo buckle, was forced into evening gowns, ruffles, Spandex, and giant, fluffy hair that mirrored even

© Alan L. Mayor

It takes two! Duet team Jacky Ward and Reba McEntire celebrate their joint effort at a Mercury Records party.

fluffier songs. She chafed under Mercury's insistent push into the adult-contemporary crossover market. "This wasn't at all like the kind of music I had grown up listening to and liking," she said. Her strengths and true identity—the "real Reba" from Oklahoma—were being overlooked in favor of molding her to look and sound like everybody else. However, she was not yet in a position to do anything about it, other than voice her concern. "Nobody wanted me to do the kind of stuff I'm best at. I felt like a fish out of water."

The record executives seemed determined to stifle her individuality, constantly trying to shape her into whatever had already worked commercially. As a result, Reba had her Loretta Lynn style, her Patsy Cline style, her Dolly Parton style. All along, Jackie McEntire was the only one encouraging Reba to develop her own distinctive style, something true to her background. Says an appreciative Reba about her role-model mother, "It was good advice, and I really did work hard to sing my way—from the heart."

6 THE BEGINNING OF THE "REBA" DECADE

One interesting way to look at the recent history of country music is to divide it into periods represented by its most influential female artists. From the '50s through the '70s, Patsy Montana, Molly O'Day, Kitty Wells, Patsy Cline, Loretta Lynn, and Tammy Wynette ruled the day. But the 1980s was most certainly the decade of Reba McEntire, as she climbed to the top of the heap. The '70s had been a bad time for Nashville. Crossover mania had ultimately failed. The record companies had lost money, and the decade ended with massive firings in 1979. Reba would play a major role in reviving Nashville, giving it a new direction that would insure its importance as a musical center beyond the next decade.

Success came slowly to McEntire in the early part of the '80s. Nobody was really shocked in the summer of 1980, when Reba finally had a hit single, "(You Lift Me) Up to Heaven," which stayed on the charts until August. As in riding a bucking bronco, she just had to sit tight and wait for enough people to hear her amazing voice. "Up to Heaven" provided the breakthrough.

McEntire's third album, *Feel the Fire,* was released in October 1980. The cover photograph, shot through a haze of pink light and slightly out-of-focus, shows a very young and soft Reba wearing iridescent makeup and a filmy dress. She dedicated the album to her new husband: "I sang this one for Charlie. Love, Reba McEntire."

The standout single on the album, "(You Lift Me) Up to Heaven," is a western swing tune—an inspirational song with so much emotion that it sends chills up and down the spine of the listener, a frequent experience with Reba McEntire! Accompanied by a twangy country guitar and backed by too many strings and distracting background vocals (the style of the day), Reba sings about a love so strong and exciting it can lift her spirits higher than the Colorado mountains. In true country tradition (it's a man's world), the boyfriend is praised for providing heaven on earth, for making life worth living.

As in riding a bucking bronco, she just had to sit tight and wait for enough people to hear her amazing voice. "Up to Heaven" provided the breakthrough.

Although "(You Lift Me) Up to Heaven" was the standout hit of the album, a number of other tracks were squarely in the mold of the newly emerging Reba McEntire style. "Tears on My Pillow," an old Smokey Robinson song from the early Motown era, is all about heartbreak. A jilted woman, in this case, wants her lover back—she'll do anything to make it so. Reba's style on this one is very reminiscent of Loretta Lynn, but says McEntire, "If people say I sound like Loretta—that's all right with me! I take that as a real compliment."

Another western number, "I Don't Think Love Ought to Be That Way," has a woman telling a prospective lover that she doesn't want to be a one-night stand—she has higher expectations. "Long Distance Lover" is a tear-jerking ballad. The long-distance lover, calling from Memphis, just can't seem to make that all-important commitment, so the object of his affections, a sad woman who has taken all she can, is leaving rather than be used anymore. From now on, his calls to her will reach a phone that rings in an empty room.

"If I Had My Way" has a traditional country theme—that of a love affair with a married man, a woman who is tired of having only stolen moments of love filled with lies.

"I Can See Forever in Your Eyes" was another single from the album that made it onto the charts, but not very high and not for long. It is in the style that many Reba fans love best—western swing, which is her true heritage. This is an upbeat song about a woman so in love—so happy and so protected by her lover—that she has only an even more wonderful future to look forward to. This is what dreams are made of!

"A Poor Man's Roses (or a Rich Man's Gold)," an inspirational tune, pronounces true love worth more than any material possession, while "My Turn" has a woman taking care of the man who usually takes care of her. She wants to give something back in a very sexy way.

"Look at the One (Who's Been Looking at You)" admonishes a man who chases every skirt to love the woman who really loves him, who's always there for him. Reba tells him in a spirited, lively way to pay attention!

The final cut on the album, "Suddenly There's a Valley," is an inspirational song about good times and sad times and the things that sustain us during both. Life isn't perfect, but it will always get better. The song is filled with emotion and hope, and Re-

© Alan L. Mayor

Wynonna Judd (left) and Reba McEntire watch makeup artist Vanessa Sellers transform Statler Brother Don Reid at the *Music City News* Awards show.

© Alan L. Mayor

Harold Reid, one of the legendary Statler Brothers, offers a bear hug at a DJ reception.

© Alan L. Mayor

Singing to a seemingly endless sea of fans at Fan Fair!

ba's vocalizing is impressive. As one critic noted, "Nobody in the business can take a note through so many twists and turns, wringing out the last drop of emotion before turning it loose and leaving the listeners on the edges of their seats, waiting for the next syllable."

Having a bona-fide hit under her belt gave Reba confidence that her career was on its way up, though it would be almost a year before she had another really big single release. That summer, the Battles' decided to splurge on their dream house and bought a 215-acre ranch in Stringtown, Oklahoma (population 500), not too far from Reba's hometown and her family. Situated with a view of

A devoted crowd vies for a chance to press some famous flesh!

Chockie Mountain, the ranch was three hours from the nearest airport. Travel had not yet become a major factor in Reba's life, however—she typically had only one or two singing dates a month in those days. Most of her time was spent around the ranch, helping Charlie. Together they raised 1,200 head of Brahman and Hereford cattle for market.

Ranching and Charlie's rodeo winnings for the most part supported the young couple in those days. Battles also acted as his wife's personal manager. Neither of them had any idea at the time just how Reba's career would take off, changing both their lives—and eventually their marriage. It was a relatively peaceful time for Reba, who vowed she

Reba introduces her first husband, Charlie Battles (right), to Grant Turner, dean of the Grand Ole Opry announcers.

would never leave the Sooner state. "I don't need to live in Nashville to work there," she said. "I hope I never have to leave Oklahoma."

Charlie's sons were often in residence at the Stringtown ranch. Reba, intent (okay—obsessed!) on furthering her career, voiced little interest in having a family of her own then, even though her brother and sisters were all beginning to have children. She joked that after one particular visit by all her nieces and nephews, she ran into the bathroom and ate "an entire package of birth control pills!"

Reba didn't know it then, of course, but her cowgirl days were numbered. As she grew more and more famous, Charlie banned her from helping around the ranch. "He says I might hurt the horses and cattle, but I think he's more worried that I might break my arm, and not be able to hold a microphone!"

When Reba wasn't on the road, she was playing housewife—cooking and decorating, reading romance novels, even trying her hand at oil painting, specializing in (what else?) western scenes. The Battles' marriage was a very strong joint venture in

1980, and both of them were sure it would last forever.

Jerry Kennedy produced every one of Reba's albums during her seven-year stint at Mercury. It was his job to find the right songs for Reba to record, although he wanted to make sure that she was comfortable with each cut. They usually agreed on the selections, although both were bound by what was "in" on the Nashville scene at the time. Reba considered herself lucky that Jerry was so agreeable to work with. She was a long way from artistic freedom, but she knew she wanted it and had every intention of getting it.

In 1981, Reba McEntire made it onto the country charts with three hit singles: "I Don't Think Love Ought to Feel That Way," from *Feel the Fire,* and "Today All Over Again" and the '50s oldie from the Platters, "Only You (and You Alone)"—both off the *Heart to Heart* album, released that year.

Heart to Heart includes a ballad Reba sings with Ricky Skaggs, but most of the songs revolve around a woman's need for a good man—a decidedly nonfeminist sentiment, though that would change soon. "Women in rock and pop music had always had a strong voice and a strong message. Country music was lagging behind, but it would catch up—and soon," said Jimmy Bowen, speaking of that period in Reba's career.

By the end of 1982, Reba had hit paydirt—one of her singles, "Can't Even Get the Blues No More," hit number one on the *Billboard* country chart. Her interest in pop singers Donna Summer and Sheena Easton may have accounted for her choice of such a heavily pop/rock-influenced song about love go-

© A. J. Pantsios/London Features

She don't want no cheatin' men—and that means you!

ing so sour that she was getting numb to it. The background vocals (including Reba's sister Susie) are so "pop" that they remind one of the Ray Charles' Raylettes from the '60s.

Reba remembers how she found the song that finally skyrocketed her to the top of the charts. "Jerry Kennedy and I were listening to some tapes between shows I was doing with Mickey Gilley. I just loved 'Can't Even Get the Blues No More,' and we put it in the 'maybe' stack. Jerry told me that this one might not be my style, and I said that's funny, because I haven't really found my style yet. Nothing is really consistent with me—I think maybe *that's* my style. I can't keep doing the same thing over and over—I'll get bored. Now the songwriters have figured it out and are sending me lots of different things. I like doing slow waltzes and the ballads, but this song was just so different—a real pick-me-up. I'm a country and western singer and I always will be, but I love to sing just about anything."

Two of the cuts on Reba McEntire's next album, *Unlimited*, were definitely in the Dolly Parton vibrato mode—not totally unexpected inasmuch as, during that era, Dolly had become a crossover dream complete with million-selling records and starring roles in movies and television. Even Reba's cover photo echoed Dolly—a very sophisticated and glamorous pose, a dress covered in silver-blue sequins, and hair that was getting bigger by the hour.

"You're the First Time I've Thought About Leaving," the other song from the album that made it onto the charts in a big way, has an old-fashioned country flavor. Loaded with steel pedal guitar, it's a song about a woman who should leave her lover because the relationship just isn't working, but she lacks the resolve and strength it's going to take. The other Dolly-like song, "Whoever's Watchin'," depicts a girl who's better off than ever, figuring somebody "up there" is keeping an eye out for her.

On "I'd Say You," a woman praises the man who is everything to her. Love and emotion practically ooze from Reba's powerful voice. "Everything I'll Ever Own" is a ballad about a love lost, and is overpowered (as is much of the album) by string arrangements so dense that anybody other than Reba would have been lost in the noise.

"What Do You Know About Heartache?" is a gutsy, up-tempo tune about a broken-hearted man looking for a shoulder to cry on. The girl he goes to

© A. J. Barratt/Retna Ltd.

Outside the Crazy Horse Saloon, the perfect setting for a country gal from Oklahoma.

for sympathy challenges his depth of feeling; she is suffering far more than he is, since she is in love with him and he doesn't even notice! "Out of the Blue" is a mellow, easy-listening song about falling in love unexpectedly. It's easy to see and worth noting that the hit songs Reba had from this album had much more to do with her singing than the quality of the compositions themselves.

A gal is not going to take it anymore from a cruel lover in "Over, Under and Around"—she's over him, not under his spell anymore, and not planning to be around to try love with him a second time. "I'm Not That Lonely Yet" has a similar theme—even though the girl's depressed, she can muster up the strength to break away from her good-for-nothing boyfriend.

Back-to-back hits, "Can't Even Get the Blues No More" and "You're the First Time I've Thought

About Leaving" made a statement loud and clear: Miss Reba McEntire had arrived! Reba was in seventh heaven. Her quest for a number one song had taken six years instead of the five originally predicted by Red Steagall, but it was "well worth the wait!" declared the new star.

As evidence of Reba's elevated status, she appeared on the "Tonight Show" with Johnny Carson, and while in Hollywood, auditioned for small parts on prime-time TV shows. There was a gig singing at the Orange Bowl on New Year's Eve, and with a newly expanded "recognition factor," Reba was opening for big-time country acts like the Statler Brothers and Ronnie Milsap. She even got some bookings in Las Vegas. Life was becoming a thrill a minute, even if it meant being constantly on the road.

© Kevin Winter/DMI

Rodeo Reba shows off her big belt buckle and her western wear—befitting the leader of the neotraditionalist movement in country music.

The Nashville Network (TNN), still in its early days, featured Reba often in 1983. Ralph Emery, known as the "King of Nashville" and recently recognized by *T.V. Guide* as "country music's most influential figure for someone who doesn't sing or play an instrument," was just getting his talk show off the ground, and Reba stopped by often for a chat. She also appeared on several variety shows in that era—"Hee Haw," "Nashville After Hours," "Nashville Alive," and the sitcom "I-40 Paradise."

That summer, Reba was inducted into the Walkway of the Stars in the Country Music Hall of Fame during Fan Fair, a huge, circuslike annual event on the fairgrounds in Nashville. For country music fans, Fan Fair is Nirvana. Caravans of recreational vehicles, jam-packed with rabid music lovers, arrive to celebrate in Music City under big tents and to be entertained by every major star of the genre. The faithful and adoring audiences line up for hours just to get a glimpse, and maybe an autograph, of their favorite singers. Nashville's musical royalty contributes star-studded performances and parties for the various fan clubs who have come to take part in this incredible, legendary event. Since the beginning of her career, a much beloved Reba has always been a major attraction. Her honesty, caring, and humility, not to mention a voice that slays, continue to make her a Fan Fair favorite to this day.

Along with success came a new confidence—Reba had gained acceptance. No longer was she an outsider in the Nashville music industry. With a little experience under her big, shiny "Reba" rodeo belt, Ms. McEntire focused some of her considerable energy on her stage show, which she found wanting. "I need to communicate better to the audience, and not be so self-conscious," she said at the time. "I still find myself thinking about walking across the stage in high heels." Choreography, wardrobe changes, and better lighting were things that needed improvement. "It's impossible for me to realize my dreams right now, but I've got plans," declared Reba. "I'm never satisfied. The day I am, I'll probably walk off the stage and quit!"

7 BACK TO BASICS

Even though most crossover acts in Nashville had crashed and burned during the end of the '70s, there were still plenty of success stories. The musical style of the day remained a stale, sanitized mixture of country and pop, evidencing little change or innovation in a long time. But crossover seemed the only path to big money, and not many recording executives or artists were confident enough to strike out with something different and untested. There were a handful of country purists, like Ricky Skaggs, George Strait, and Reba, who felt that their kind of music—rooted in tradition and true to their rural heritage—was what the people wanted, if only the Nashville establishment would take a chance and find out.

The bottom line, as always in business, was economics. Nashville would resist any kind of change so long as the stars who set the standards—Eddie Rabbitt, Hank Williams, Jr., Dolly Parton, and Barbara Mandrell—continued to rake in major dollars,

© Beth Gwinn/Retna, Ltd.

Fighting the male chauvinist powers of Nashville, Reba blazes the trail to bring back traditional country music.

rule the airwaves, and attract the attention of the national press. Around this time, Barbara Mandrell and her sisters had their own highly rated and visible weekly variety show on national television. When Barbara built a huge glass and log house the size of a football field outside of Nashville, *People* magazine was right there to cover it. She was the envy and role model of every woman singer coming out of Music City in that era.

"The beginning of the 1980s was almost the end of country music," said superstar Ricky Skaggs, one of the first to buck the Nashville system in order to spearhead the "new-traditionalist" move-

"Let the music lift you up"—and up and up!

© Beth Gwinn/Retna Ltd.

ment. "As a music form, it was thrown onto the garbage heap," recounted Dwight Yoakum, whose smoldering good looks and style made him a crossover star without his having to change his musical style. "It's tragic that we ignored ethnic American music for so long."

Skaggs led the push for change. "Musically, country got so sterile and syrupy, with all those intense string arrangements and background singing. It was so Las Vegas. I knew what country was, and I wasn't hearing it on the radio at all." Ricky, universally credited with the great popularity of the new country credo, "Say It Loud, We're Crackers and We're Proud!", forced the issue when he singlehandedly returned to back-to-basics country tradition—bluegrass, honky-tonk, rockabilly, western swing.

Unable to stem the tide of "middle-of-the-road mush" that was the staple of country radio, Ricky Skaggs worked hard to prove that old-fashioned country and western music was what the people wanted—that it was commercially and critically viable for the Nashville music industry. "We listened to the average fan. They wanted the real thing, and we gave it to them."

Skaggs was eventually joined by Yoakum, George Strait, Randy Travis, and Reba McEntire, who asked, "If everybody likes it, why aren't we doing it?"

By the middle of 1983, Reba McEntire had made a fateful decision. She was about to leave Mercury, having signed a new deal with MCA Records, famous as the label that owned Decca, home of Patsy Cline and Loretta Lynn. This change would herald the Golden Age of Reba. Though it didn't happen right away, MCA would boost McEntire to her first gold album. The label would create an atmosphere for peak creativity, a place for Reba to flex her business muscles, send a message to her music sisters, win a lifetime of awards, and skyrocket her career into the cosmos.

Earlier in the year, Irving Azoff had been named president of MCA. Azoff, diminutive but much feared in Los Angeles, where he ruled because of his hard-driving negotiating talents, had discovered and managed (in the '70s) the Eagles, Jackson Browne, and Linda Ronstadt. He was also a talented movie producer with a good track record, responsible for *Urban Cowboy* and its attendant frenzy (though the cowboy craze had died out in Nashville—if you saw somebody wearing the total cowboy look around town, chances were he was from Ohio!), and the movie that made Sean Penn a name before he became Mr. Madonna—*Fast Times at Ridgemont High.*

Immediately following his appointment as head of MCA, Azoff announced that the usually conservative country division would be expanding aggressively. He was one of the first executives who

Performing with fellow country neotraditionalist Randy Travis.

© Steve Lowry/Nashville Banner

Reba with country superstar Lee Greenwood.

© Alan L. Mayor

saw Music City for the gold mine it has become—country music, once the poor cousin of the record business, now grosses over $8 billion a year! Bringing Reba McEntire into the MCA fold was Azoff's way of saying that country would make big money, and that Reba was going to be one of the biggest stars in the new order of things. Not only did he love her voice, he also had vision and was a true believer!

Just before Reba announced her new record deal at a splashy party, Mercury came out with her sixth album, *Behind the Scene.* To help her publicize it, Reba hired a promotion company for the first time, Network Ink. With true celebrity status within her reach, Reba decided it was time for a media blitz to keep her on the fast track to stardom. Having been bitten by the bug, she wanted more, to be top dog, "as big as the guys"—something that seemed against all odds at that point in country music, for while there were popular female country stars—and a history of "Country Music Queens," men still very much ruled the day.

Reba did garner a nomination for her first Coun-

Reba belts out some real old-fashioned country.

try Music Award. Though she didn't win, she felt she was on her way. ICM was hired to book her live shows, keeping her on the road constantly, often on the bill with other major names—at MGM Grand in Las Vegas with the Statlers and with Conway Twitty, the Judds, and George Strait. It was heaven, even though it was hard work. "The rodeo prepared me for the music business—traveling and meeting people. It's natural to me by now."

Behind the Scene lacked a hit single, but it was well received and favorably reviewed. The album once again featured a glamorous Reba on the cover, and the musical selections were largely predictable, but did include one of McEntire's own compositions, "Reasons," which she had written on her ranch in Oklahoma. A standout song on the LP was a waltz, "There Ain't No Future in This"—about a wandering man who's never going to live up to his promises, no matter how sincere he sounds. The music and lyrics are deceptively simple, yet the critics compared Reba's dramatic delivery to Edith Piaf. "In less than two and a half minutes, McEntire swings from tender resignation to resentment against her lover's past and still dominant love to a simple wail at her hopeless situation," wrote one critic. "As the shattering outburst of her last high note cascades into a subsiding coloratura reprise of the title line, one has to say that Reba is a genius."

"Nickel Dreams" is about a girl who makes it in her career but has an emotional life that is nothing to write home about. She catches her man cheating in "One Good Reason," and hopes her sacrifices for true love pay off in "You Better Love Me After This." As usual, there was one rock and roll–type tune on the album, "Why Do We Want What We

"As the shattering outburst of her last high note cascades into a subsiding coloratura reprise of the title line, one has to say that Reba is a genius."

Know We Can't Have," but Reba deflected critics who worried she was getting too far from the fold. "I'll always be country," she assured them.

Reba left Mercury behind but did it graciously and with class. "Mercury was great to me. They kept me for eight years when they could have easily kicked me out after the second album—'cause I wasn't selling. I had some great teachers over there, but now it's time to do something new."

Jim Foglesong was the head of MCA Nashville when Reba signed her new deal with them. To Reba, starting out fresh at a new label meant change all around. Represented by agent Don Williams (singer Andy's brother) while at Mercury, McEntire chose to sign on with Bill Carter, a well-connected former Secret Service agent who had been heavily involved with the Rolling Stones since the early 1970s. Carter was also instrumental in David Bowie's career, running his 1983 World Tour, functioning as the executive producer on Bowie's HBO special, and packaging his "Asia in Asia" show for MTV.

Under the new arrangement, husband Charlie Battles was relegated to handling only a portion of the bookings, making him much less involved with Reba's management than he had been before.

Reba's first release on MCA was *Just a Little Love,* produced by Norro Wilson, a man both Reba and Charlie were enchanted with. Being allowed to hand-pick her own producer was stipulated in Reba's new MCA contract. McEntire's new work garnered major press attention. *The New Yorker* called the effort "an unburdening of Reba's voice," with songs perfect to showcase her intense soprano. Stylistically, the record is mixed—waltzes, country-flavored ballads, swing, a bit of rock—but every song is about love. The album was not all that different from Reba's last few records on Mercury, but the production values were definitely a step up. Most important of all, however, Reba now had more power over her career, bolstering her confidence, giving her a new assurance that reflected in her soaring voice. The album cover features a very demure Reba dressed in a soft white sweater and diamonds. Both Steve Wariner and Vince Gill appear on the record with her.

The title cut is as sweet as Reba's picture on the cover. She praises her lover for making her feel safe, secure, and wanted in a crazy world, a man able to cancel out all the negativity swirling around trouble at work, bills to pay, a world at war—all with a little love and affection.

"Poison Sugar" is a country pop tune about a tall, dark, and dangerous man—a "love thief" with poison on his lips. His passion will suck a girl in, but he's a liar, and eventually she'll find herself waking up alone. "I'm Gettin' Over You" is about a woman who has changed her life around in an effort to forget the man who is no longer a part of her life—she's bought new clothes, redecorated the house, takes his name off the mailbox, and is learning to do new things. She's still hurting, but the bad feeling will be over soon.

Producer Norro Wilson is the coauthor of the ballad "You Are Always There for Me." A woman expresses gratitude to her lover, who is patient, forgiving, offers guidance, and is always strong in adversity. Most of all, he's a good friend.

Sounding a lot like Pat Benatar, Reba belts out a trite little ditty, "Every Second Someone Breaks a Heart," which elevates a broken heart into a national emergency.

Reba now had more power over her career, bolstering her confidence, giving her a new assurance that reflected in her soaring voice.

Two of the cuts on the album are reminiscent of Loretta Lynn at her best. "Tell Me What's So Good About Goodbye" is a song about disappointment. A woman thought love would last forever, but now it has come to an end. She contemplates her situation sadly—all that's left behind are "tattered dreams and broken memories." The end of love is so hard to forget.

"He Broke Your Memory Last Night" is more upbeat. She thought she'd never fall in love again, and kept memories of her previous love locked away as if they were fine china or crystal. Then, when she least expects it, a new man comes along and she falls in love with him, and the memories of the old love just aren't important anymore.

"If Only" is a heartbreaking song full of regrets. If only she had told him she loved him more, hadn't taken him for granted and tried a little harder. If only she'd held him closer, hadn't pretended things weren't going wrong—maybe they could have avoided the saddest thing in the world—saying goodbye.

"Congratulations" is yet another song about broken romance, its ironic lyrics set to a waltz. She believed she was his only love, but he sure showed her—stealing her heart and then tearing her world apart. "Silver Eagle" is a lively swing number with some wild fiddling, so lavishly produced that Reba's voice is almost obscured, though it's a catchy tune about all kinds of freedom.

After *Just a Little Love* came out, Jimmy Bowen was newly installed as the head of MCA. Bowen, who became known as the "Svengali of Nashville with the Midas touch," had a burning desire to build country music into a healthy, mass-market business. This passion was something he shared with the woman who would become his protege, Reba McEntire.

Jimmy Bowen came from Texas, where he learned to sing and play the bass guitar. "I hated country music when I grew up—I was a rock and roller all the way," he remembers now. Starting out in the music business in 1956 as an artist/writer, he traveled with Alan Freed's legendary Rock and Roll Show tour, starring Jerry Lee Lewis, on which many of the Motown stars, among whom Diana Ross and the Supremes, got their start.

Jimmy went to L.A. in 1963 to work for Reprise, Frank Sinatra's record company. Bowen not only produced "That's Life" and "Strangers in the Night" for Ole Blue Eyes, he also produced Dean Martin at the height of that star's popularity (and beyond), including "Everybody Loves Somebody." "I was seriously into the pop scene in the sixties and seventies, working with people like Sammy Davis, Jr., and Kenny Rogers and the First Edition," says Bowen.

With a little direction, Bowen realized, Nashville could be a gold mine. He relocated there, working for a series of record companies—MGM, Elektra Asylum, Warner Bros., and finally MCA—and helped direct the careers of Hank Williams, Jr., Conway Twitty, and Crystal Gayle, among others. A free-thinking, enlightened man, Bowen was the

Jimmy Bowen once produced records for "Ole Blue Eyes" and is currently president of Capitol Nashville. It was Bowen who urged McEntire to take charge of her own career and address herself to the emotions and interests of women.

perfect partner for a revolutionary Reba, who declared herself a neo-traditionalist at a time when almost nobody was singing old-fashioned country and western music. Reba knew she was country, and that's what she wanted to be, not an imitation of someone else—Streisand, Summer, or any of the crop of current pop divas. Some people thought she was crazy and was cutting her career short. But not Jimmy Bowen.

More than anything else, Reba McEntire wanted to be herself—to go back to her Oklahoma roots both in her music and her image. She planned to make an album that would, once and for all, shake the pop influences she had labored under for so long and with such modest success. Reba wanted to record old standards, filled with lots of steel pedal guitar, fiddles, and honest emotions about universal themes. She put together a tape of some of her favorite classic country tunes, with cuts by Ray Price, Merle Haggard, Patsy Cline, and Loretta Lynn, just to get a feel for what she wanted to accomplish with her next album. "Country music has gotten awful diluted these days," announced the strong-minded McEntire. "I'd like to see it get back to the way it was. I'm going to do some politicking to get rid of all those strings, synthesizers, and horns."

Reba's next album for MCA, *My Kind of Country*, was already in the works. Looking to do a bold mix of music that didn't mask her incredible voice or her rich heritage, she was hooked up with the phenomenally successful producer Harold Shedd, who'd put the group Alabama on the road to superstardom. Reba was having trouble finding original songs that fit her new purist-country leanings. Much of what was being pitched her way by the top songwriters was still crossover, and she just wasn't buying.

The Shedd/McEntire pairing was headed for trouble—he didn't agree with her new direction and a serious conceptual difference arose. Reba kept saying she wanted steel pedal guitar and fiddles; Harold kept telling her she didn't have the right songs. Eventually, Reba took her troubles to Jimmy Bowen.

In a show of unexpected and unprecedented support, Bowen gave Reba total creative control over her record. He told her to go out and find her own songs. It was a major turning point for Reba, who would soon find herself firmly entrenched on the road to fame beyond her wildest dreams.

"When I met Reba McEntire in the early 1980s," recalls Jimmy Bowen, "she was having some radio play success, but she wasn't selling albums. She had a great voice, but she wasn't singing 'Reba' music yet. I told her that she was incredibly smart, and to take charge of her career. She should be calling the shots."

Reba, being Reba, went for it. "Jimmy was incredibly encouraging," she said. "He said, 'You know your music. You work out on the road and talk to people. Give them what you know they want and like.' "

And Bowen, unafraid to put his money where his mouth was, financed Reba's risky career move at a time that the rest of Nashville was on an austerity trip. "Because I have a big range, everybody thought I should cut contemporary stuff," said Reba. "But that's not a good reason for singing something you're not comfortable with." Luckily, her new direction turned out for the best.

It was a big breakthrough for a lone woman in the male-dominated music business, and the bril-

Taking control of her career, Reba went for a new look—western cowgirl mixed with just the right amount of glitz.
© Alan L. Mayor

liant collaboration with Bowen elevated her status and power in Nashville. Her taking control of her own career was a groundbreaking move that opened the doors to women in country music for the rest of the decade.

It was no longer a matter of just showing up to sing. Now Reba's artistic freedom was virtually unlimited, and she was involved in every aspect of making a record, even coproducing (with Bowen). "I had a thousand times more input than before. Sitting in on mixing and mastering was a first, and Jimmy didn't just tolerate me, he wanted me there." McEntire also began to be instrumental in choosing her own tunes. Soon she was listening to and considering almost a hundred songs a day.

Recording *My Kind of Country* was scary. "Nobody else was doing that kind of thing much—it really did feel like real country music was slipping away. The reason it came back is honesty. Like Ricky Scaggs. He's as honest as the day is long, and bluntly refuses to be something that he's not. He says he's not that good of an actor! It's all about who we are—country—and that's just what we're going to sing."

Reviving her "robust, rural, and determined" singing style, Reba chose a combination of oldies originally recorded by Ray Price, Carl Smith, and Faron Young, and new compositions with punch and vitality. "What I usually do is find most of the songs I'm going to record, and then I let my band learn them, and I do 'em in my stage show and live with them for a couple of months," explained Reba in her new incarnation. "Then, in the studio, when the session musicians get familiar with the song and go into the studio to lay down the instrumental tracks, I'll go in and sing with 'em. That way, they feed off me and I feed off them, and we get more feeling. I don't like to go in and just add the vocal to a prerecorded music track. I'll sing it three or four times, just in case I make a boo-boo, but we usually go with the live track—just for that extra feeling."

Unlike country music queens of yore who have known hard times and suffered hard knocks, Reba has had to borrow many of the feelings of anguish that fill her music. At this point in her career, she didn't find life hard at all, and was always explaining to fans that everything in her life was peachy. She was only pretending to feel the pain.

"The first time Harlan Howard played 'Somebody Should Leave' [which turned out to be a num-

"Sometimes the song I'm singing is so sad I just start to cry onstage."

© Alan L. Mayor

ber one single from the *My Kind of Country* album], a sad song about divorce, I cried. I've never been divorced," said Reba, still happily married to Charlie Battles at the time, "but I've been around divorce. Charlie's been, and he's got two children. It's horrible. Divorces hurt so many people—for a lifetime, not just a month or a year. My nieces and nephews have been through a divorce, and sometimes I'll get to singing that song onstage, and I'll think about them babies, remembering when they were kids, hearing the arguments, and it makes me so sad. Sometimes when I sing it, I even forget the audience is there, and just start crying."

My Kind of Country, with every song "picked with a sense of history," features a very "westernized" Reba on the cover, wearing jeans, a crisp white shirt, a fur-lined vest, and her rodeo buckle, with natural makeup and casual hair, standing in the foreground of the Rocky Mountains. Every song on the album features the unvarnished Reba, a bona fide member of the mainstream of country music. The clarity of her voice is thrilling. As befits a traditional country album, the theme is heartbreak, cheating men, living through a broken heart, and finally finding happiness with the "right one."

"How Blue" was the first single released from the album; it shot right to the top of the country charts. It is an up-tempo tune—featuring a major fiddle lead-in—with a plaintive lyric asking how blue can she be now that her lover is gone.

In the mode of Patsy Cline, "That's What He said" is a slow, sad song about a woman who's been lied to by her lover, who promised that he'd never leave but then did. With a feisty, challenging tone, "I Want to Hear It from You" features a woman demanding to know where she stands with her man.

"Sometimes when I sing it, I even forget the audience is there, and just start crying."

Their love may be over, and he may have found someone new, but he'd better tell her so to her face—she doesn't want to learn her fate secondhand.

"It's Not Over (If I'm Not Over You)" is a woman's lament to the man who done her wrong. He may think their relationship is over, but it's not, because she's still in love with him and he'll always be a part of her.

The absolute tearjerker of the lot, and the album's biggest hit, is "Somebody Should Leave." Reba's superb voice is so overwhelmed with emotion that it hits the affected listener right between the eyes. The song is all about divorce. Two people who were once happy are faced with their dying love, and they just can't bear to discuss what needs talking about—one of them will have to leave. The biggest problem is the babies—their father needs them, and they need their mama. There's a lot of crying and pain that will go on and on. It's a very strong song, perfectly rendered by Reba in a direct, unadorned style befitting the emotion of the lyrics.

"Everything But My Heart," with another lyric about love gone sour, is a pop-flavored song in which Reba gets to flex her vocal muscles. More in the true western swing tradition, "Don't You Believe Him" warns another woman that even though her new boyfriend is a sweet talker and can give a gal a reason to live, he's a cheatin' man who'll lie when it suits him, and if she believes him, then he'll leave her, too.

Even though love isn't perfect, it's thrilling. That's the spunky message of "Before I Met You." This man is good-looking and she wants him. He's made her realize that she's never really been kissed before and didn't have a clue what being truly blue was all about. The ups have never been

Reba likes to provide her audience with razzle-dazzle, otherwise "they might just as well stay home and listen to the radio."

© Beth Gwinn/Retna Ltd.

so up and the downs have never been so down. It's a roller coaster, but she loves it—and him.

Not all men will break your heart and let you down. Just the opposite is true in "He's Only Everything." He might look like an ordinary man, but to her he's everything good. His love is so special, it keeps his woman safe and happy.

"You've Got Me (Right Where You Want Me)" is a plaintive song about a woman who's in the palm of her man's hand. He's got her right where he wants her, and while she knows it, she can't resist. She's just hoping and praying that he doesn't abuse the privilege!

After the "no more crossover" edict, Reba's star was on the rise. Now that the music had changed, a new look was in order as well. As reflected on the cover of *My Kind of Country,* Reba chose to go for a "chic western mode." To help make the change to a viable country purist, Diana Eden, a costumer from Los Angeles whose credits included creations for Cher and Diana Ross, was brought in to design outfits that would go with the famous "Reba" belt buckle. It called for something earthy to highlight Reba's famous titian tresses, yet flashy (but not too flashy) and a little sexy—like sequined blouses and patchwork skirts accented with lace. "I'm going for the modern western woman outfit—an updated version of Barbara Stanwyck as Victoria Barkley from *Big Valley*!" Reba joked.

To make her stage show more sophisticated, lighting designer Allen Branton, known for his work with the Rolling Stones, Asia, and the Oak Ridge Boys, was brought in, and several choreographers were imported from L.A. to make Reba's stage moves look effortless.

BREAKING RECORDS 8

Appearing at the 1984 Country Music Association Awards show, Reba McEntire was vindicated for her true country leanings. *My Kind of Country* became her biggest commercial and artistic success so far. Once Reba took control of her destiny, stopped listening to what everybody else said, and determined to be true to herself, her career soared into the wide open spaces.

On the CMA show, hosted by Kenny Rogers and broadcast nationally on CBS TV, Reba won the first of her four consecutive (1984–1987) "Female Artist of the Year" awards. This is a highly prestigious feat no other artist has ever accomplished. Country female legends Loretta Lynn and Tammy Wynette had each won three awards before their own runs ended.

This first awards night started out as a nightmare, however. Reba hated how she looked, and ran around backstage trying to get herself together. She was by no means sure she'd win. Just the opposite. "I can be very insecure!" she has confessed. In the end, though, it was a memorable evening. After her name was announced as the winner, Reba, with tears in her eyes, dedicated her prize to her mother, who had helped her to fulfill her dream. "My momma and daddy are my role models—they never started anything they didn't finish and finish well," she said.

Winning her first CMA Award was a major high, but Reba also wanted to get in her two cents about the show, which featured a lot of pop material. There were performances by Dolly Parton, Ray Charles, B. J. Thomas, Bill Medley (of the Righteous Brothers), and Alabama, and the highlight was a surprise duet between popmeister Lionel Richie and Kenny Rogers of the latter's chart-busting single "Lady," causing the crowd jammed into the Grand Ole Opry to go wild with applause. A Nashville record executive explained, "The network wanted the pop influence to keep the national ratings respectable." This emphasis on pop rankled a critical McEntire: "I sure would have liked to see Conway Twitty and Hank Williams, Jr., as guest stars. Or Merle Haggard. I was thrilled to death to see Waylon Jennings."

It did not escape Reba's (or anyone's) attention that Richie received the only standing ovation of the night. "If Loretta Lynn had walked onstage at the Grammys under similar circumstances," observed Reba, "I bet nobody would have stood up for her." Yet while the "country faction" was angry that the show was so pop-flavored, it sent a strong message that popular music was a means to massive recognition, money, and power that country was not yet privy to. This experience would have a direct influence on Reba McEntire's career plans a few years down the road.

After winning the coveted CMA Award, it was easier for McEntire to fill concert halls. She no longer had to play livestock shows, rodeos, or small clubs. "I found out I was allergic to smoke and dust, so I'd have had to quit those gigs anyway," said a relieved Reba. In great demand, her bigger shows were being booked up to six months in advance—a new experience Reba greatly enjoyed and had looked forward to!

Instead of getting a big ego or going "Hollywood," Reba's success made her work that much harder, always striving to do better, "thankful to God" that her transition had been a wise decision. "When people come to see Reba McEntire and the Chockie Mountain Band, I want to be able to really dazzle them, to give them their hard-earned money's worth," she said at the time. This is the kind of sentiment that has kept (and still keeps) her fans so devoted.

Back home in Oklahoma, life was different now that Reba was a star. But, as further proof that her humility was sincere, she vowed her normal routine wouldn't change that much. "When I go home, I'm a neighbor, not a professional singer. Oh sure, when I go down to the Wal-Mart, I usually end up signin' some autographs, and people stop to talk to me. But it's not like jumpin' up and down or screamin' or anything like that. We're neighbors and that's real nice. I'm just the girl next door, and that makes me feel real good!"

In 1985, the stage was set for Reba to really take off. CMA "Entertainer of the Year" was the prize she was working toward, and she wouldn't have to wait too long for it! Traveling all over the country, McEntire performed her stage show, a blend of Las Vegas flash and down-home folksiness. Her yearly

"When I go down to the Wal-Mart, I usually end up signin' some autographs, and people stop to talk to me. But it's not like jumpin' up and down or screamin' or anything like that. We're neighbors and that's real nice."

release, *Have I Got a Deal for You*, was the first album that had Reba McEntire listed (along with Jimmy Bowen) as executive producer. The record also had the distinction of being Nashville's first totally digital release.

Brother Pake McEntire sang "blood harmony" on the record, which featured two Reba McEntire original songs, attesting to her new confidence in her abilities. Reba has remarked that gathering material for the album was, in many ways, a bigger job than singing the songs. "I went out and listened for songs, then I put all the tapes, including the ones I had written, together in the order for an album sequence. When Jimmy [Bowen] and I was listening to 'em together, he said, 'I like "She's the One Loving You" because of the tempo.' I said, 'You really like it? Me and David Anthony and Leigh Reynolds [the guitarists in her band] wrote it.' Then my song, the one I wrote alone, "Only in My Mind," came on. Jimmy said, 'Good chorus.' I said, 'Okay—I wrote that,' and he told me he was proud of me. It wasn't like, oh well, if you wrote it, everybody'll think that's the only reason we recorded it. Because Jimmy gave me the okay before I told him it was mine, I had the guts to put it in. I felt pretty good about the whole thing."

Have I Got a Deal for You is every bit as country as her previous disc. It features harmonies that are evocative of Tammy Wynette and vocal vibrato á la Dolly Parton, along with the prerequisite "soaring" steel guitar and "mercurial" fiddling. Reba comes across stronger than ever and well on her way to being an independent woman.

"I'm in Love All Over Again" is a funky, country rocker about the joys of love when it's working. "She's Single Again," an "instant country classic," is about a lowdown, man-stealing woman on the prowl. "The Great Divide" explores the gulf between two people who just can't get it together, while the title song offers up the singer's heart so cheaply to the man she loves that there's no way he could pass up the deal. "Red Roses (Won't Work Now)" is a warning to the guy who's pushed her too far this time.

"Only in My Mind," Reba's first noncollaborative songwriting effort, has a woman thinking about cheating on her man, even though she hasn't done it yet. "She's the One Loving You Now," the other Reba tune on the album, rehashes a lost romance. "Just leave me alone to suffer" is the message in "Whose Heartache Is This Anyway?" The western-swing "I Don't Need Nothin' You Ain't Got" proves that money can't buy you love—so who needs it! The last song on the record, folksy "Don't Forget Your Way Back Home," reminds an errant lover where he belongs.

Close friends Loretta Lynn and Emmylou Harris wrote the liner notes for *Have I Got a Deal for You*, at Reba's request. "They're two of my favorites—I just about bawled when I read what they wrote—it was so sweet!"

The album cover, shot in L.A., shows Reba in a dress, alone. "It's just me. I finally got a chance to do something that's just me. I'm really tickled by it." *Rolling Stone* pronounced Reba's latest effort promising, calling the singer "sassy, self-confident, daring and expressive," without a trace of the quaintness often connected to a country thrush.

For the first time, Reba was happy with her band, her material, and her control. "I started taking time

"I started taking time to find out about all those little things that are important to me—why the bus air stinks, who's driving at three o'clock in the morning, why the lights weren't working quite right on our third song, why aren't we booked anywhere this weekend?"

to find out about all those little things that are important to me—why the bus air stinks, who's driving at three o'clock in the morning, why the lights weren't working quite right on our third song, why aren't we booked anywhere this weekend?"

If imitation is the sincerest form of flattery, Reba must have been bowled over when Loretta Lynn, returning to recording after a three-year hiatus, made an album very reminiscent of one of Reba's—right down to using Jimmy Bowen and his Lynwood Productions as her producer.

Everybody loves an award, especially Reba McEntire, who was nominated for many in 1985, a banner year for her by all accounts. She'd been working hard and had brought country back where it belonged, showing the world it could be done with great style. For the second year in a row, McEntire was honored as the Country Music Association's "Female Vocalist of the Year," though "Entertainer of the Year" went to good friend Ricky Skaggs.

Poised to be Nashville's next superstar in an era when country record executives were openly skeptical about their female acts, the second consecutive win was especially stunning. A proud and jubilant Reba accepted her award, thanking God, and also Jimmy Bowen, for letting her do her kind of music. Reba and her neo-traditionalist cohorts proved their instincts were right on the money, and the CMA Awards show reflected this with the theme "good, old country." The show featured a nod to Patsy Cline and performances by Loretta Lynn, Johnny Cash, and Merle Haggard.

The Academy of Country Music, based in Hollywood, offered an award to Reba as "Best Female Vocalist" a short time later, while, in an embarrassment of riches, *Music City News* named her "Female Artist of the Year." As if all those trophies weren't enough, *Rolling Stone*, in their annual Critic's Choice Poll, listed McEntire among their Top Five Country Artists. She was the only female included. How did the saucy redhead celebrate? She put in her own private phone at the ranch in Stringtown. "We've been on a party line all our life, so it was real exciting!"

In the wake of all this public attention, Reba practically caused a riot among revelers and devoted fans at Fan Fair 1985. Her performance was a show to remember, prompting local music critics to call her "the female voice of this generation." Pretty much everyone agreed that Reba was one of the greatest (if not *the* greatest) country singers in history.

Onstage at Fan Fair, Reba's voice dripped passion, and her eye-catching stage show had been honed to perfection. Into her fancy, country-girl mode, McEntire was all dolled up in a ruffled blouse and lace tights, prompting one wag to dub her the "modest Madonna." Most important, and a true sign of Reba's nature, she treated her fans like royalty. Closing the set with a medley of gospel tunes, Reba left the stage to a roaring standing ovation.

In her home state, it was time for even more celebration. Miss McEntire was welcomed back as everybody's favorite Okie gal. In her hometown of Kiowa, the town honored the singer and her family, even erecting a huge billboard with Reba's picture on it. In Durant, her college alma mater, Southeastern Oklahoma State, paid tribute to the school's most famous graduate over several days of organized honors.

Reba reaches out to her faithful fans.

Sunday, September 29 was pronounced "Reba McEntire Day" by the Governor of Oklahoma, George Nigh. Overwhelmed by the outpouring of love, Reba was thrilled and delighted to be back on her former campus, surrounded by old friends and McEntires. Presentations took place before and after Reba performed at a benefit concert to raise money for the school's music scholarship fund. Sharing the honors with her parents, Reba dedicated a song to them—one she and Jackie had written years before about her father.

Then came the induction as a Distinguished Alumna of Southeastern State—the highest honor that can be bestowed on a graduate. Attorney General Mike Turpen and Congressman Wes Watkins added their accolades, making Reba an Honorary Attorney General, while Charlie Battles and Pake McEntire were made Honorary Lieutenant Governors. Senator David Boren announced to the crowd that a U.S. flag was being flown over Washington, D.C., at that very moment in honor of Reba McEntire, and would be delivered directly to her when it was taken down. Earlier in the day, Reba had received a key to the city from Durant Mayor Bill Young.

The occasion wasn't all plaques and keys to the city, of course. It also provided the people of Oklahoma a chance to thank Reba publicly for her generosity. Giving both time and money, she'd shown her support for several local charities, including the Boys Ranch in Perkins and the Lions' Club Eye Banks. Reba wanted to give something back, especially to people who weren't as lucky as she was. "I've had a lot of good fortune come my way, and to be able to help people who need it makes me happy," she said.

"Emotional support makes such a difference in people's lives. When folks are as ill as some of the patients who come to Texoma Medical Center for treatment, they need all the help they can get. There's a lot of love and caring that goes into a project like this."

Since achieving her success, Reba has been involved in helping others less fortunate. For years, too, she had been recording public service spots in Nashville, distributed to more than 1,000 country radio stations, urging truckers to "buckle up." (Her efforts got her a salute from Detroit car makers.)

Perhaps closest to her heart is Reba's involvement with the Texoma Medical Center in Denison, Texas. She has raised money, mostly by performing shows down there, for a center for unwed mothers. Reba is proud to be associated with the project. "It gives girls an opportunity to continue their pregnancy rather than abort the child. It gives them an alternative. The center pays for room, board, and all medical expenses. It's a good thing." Reba has been such an effective fund-raiser, that there is now a Reba McEntire Nursery Wing down at Texoma, where Reba often visits the babies.

In the last few years, Reba has also been a spokeswoman and national chairperson of the American Lung Association Christmas Seal campaign. "This is really important, because the death rate for lung disease is growing faster than any other major disease except AIDS."

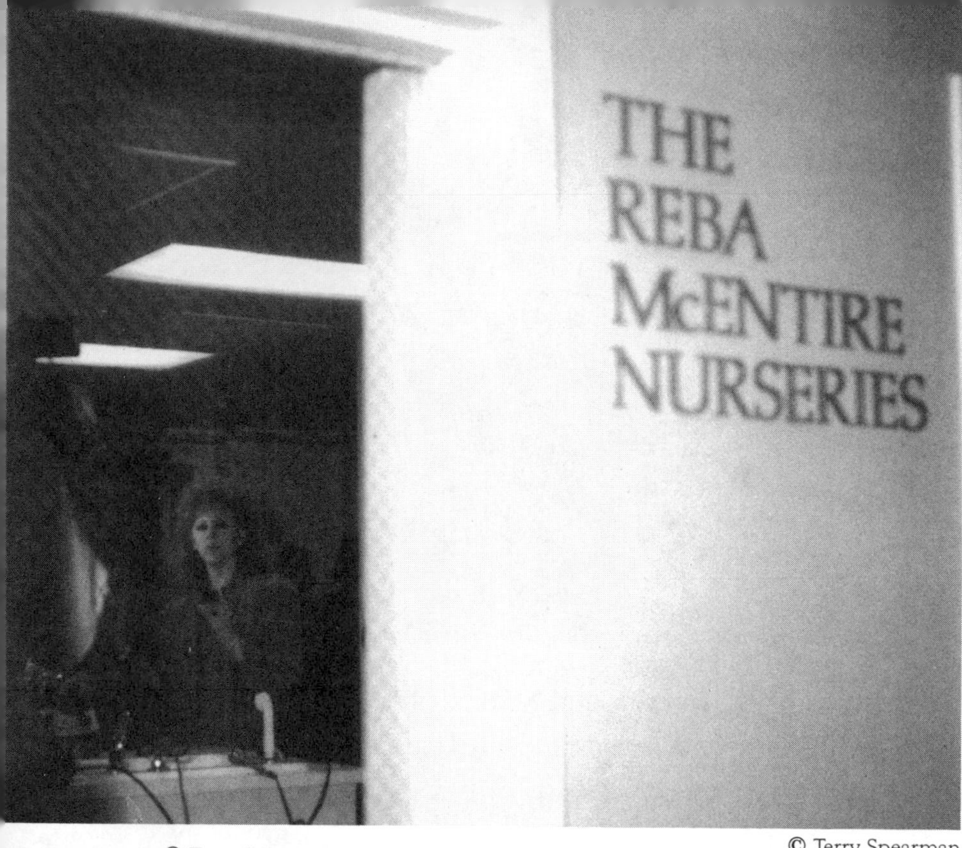

The dedication of the Reba McEntire Nurseries at the Texoma Medical Center, May 1989.

Reba meets the press and explains why her fund-raising efforts are so important to unwed mothers and their babies.

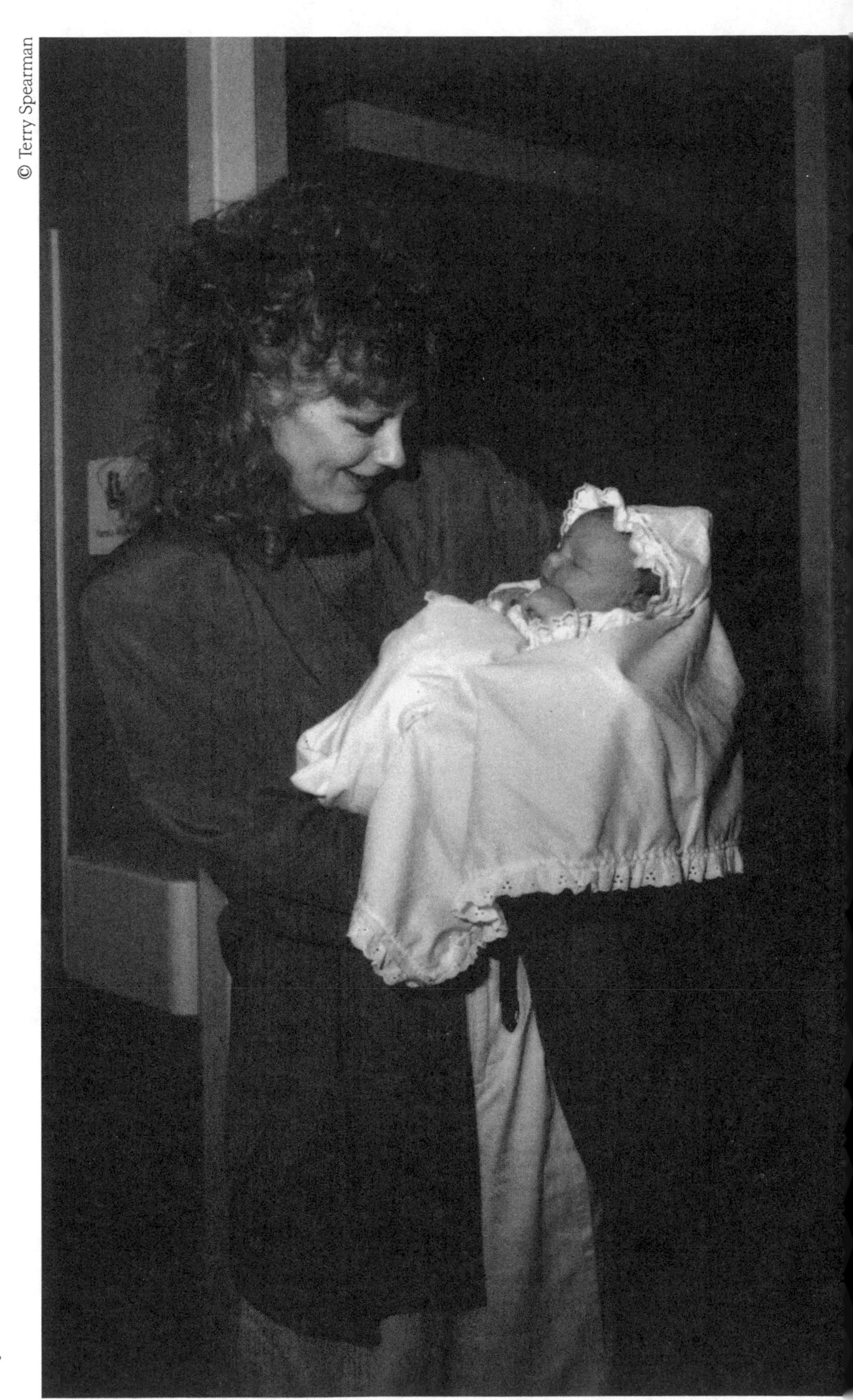

© Terry Spearman

Reba meets one of her littlest fans at the dedication of the nurseries named in her honor.

Reba has performed many benefit concerts for the Texoma Medical Center.

National Chairperson of the American Lung Association for the 1991 Christmas Seal campaign. "Christmas Seals help fund the fight against the deadly killer—lung disease."

© Terry Spearman

Courtesy of the American Lung Association

Groundbreaking ceremonies (March 27, 1991) at Texoma Medical Center for Reba's Ranchhouse, a guest house for the families of critically ill patients. Left to right: Ben Munson, Reba, Scott Smith, Jerdy Gary.

© Terry Spearman

With just enough time on her busy schedule for a quick stop in Kansas City, Reba McEntire appeared at the World Series and sang the National Anthem. With a chance to offer up more than song, this "angel of mercy" also donated blankets, pillows, and clothes to the City Union Mission.

The rewards of helping others enriched Reba's life immeasurably. As far as her career went, Reba vowed to work harder, sing better, look slicker, and rope in more and more fans. There was barely time to get home to Stringtown, though Charlie often met up with Reba on the road. One thing there wasn't time for at all—to rest on her laurels.

9 SISTERHOOD IS POWERFUL

Reba, the consummate workaholic and riding the crest of her burgeoning stardom, stayed out on the road to spread the word about her considerable talents. Manager Bill Carter urged her to get in touch with the people who sold her records—the distributors. During "Reba McEntire Month," she personally visited every major distribution company, stopping by their warehouses to shake hands with every available staff member and just generally spreading goodwill to all corners of the country. Reba even did a complete razzle-dazzle performance for Wal-Mart execs and their families. Her attention to detail paid off. Record and ticket sales soared.

Having just turned thirty, Reba decided she needed to make a change in the way she looked. She was feeling more mature, more successful, and her business savvy had made her more sophisticated. Originally, the idea was for Reba to pay a visit to her sister's haircutter, Tandy, at a local shop in McAlester, Oklahoma, just for a trim. "My hair

"When I walked out of the beauty parlor, Charlie wouldn't talk to me. He just kept looking at me and shaking his head. He finally told me he hated it, and couldn't believe I'd done that to myself."

was real long at the time—always had been," recalls Reba. Tandy talked Reba into cutting her locks short, reminding her how great Barbara Mandrell looked in her new short "do." "I thought Barbara's new haircut made her look just snazzy and real energetic, so I said—go ahead." After showing Reba a picture of what he had in mind, Tandy went to work.

"I don't know if I would have had the nerve to do it by myself. Not without asking. I guess it was a sign of growing up, being more secure, and just going and doing it," said Reba. Husband Charlie, who was off running errands in town, came back to see the results of the haircut. "When I walked out of the beauty parlor, Charlie wouldn't talk to me. He just kept looking at me and shaking his head. He finally told me he hated it, and couldn't believe I'd do that to myself. Later, he said he liked it fine."

Nineteen eighty-six turned out to be the "Year of the Gold" for the down-home diva, who won a virtual lifetime of awards in only twelve months. Reba's ability to predict what the fans wanted couldn't have been more on the mark. In the mid-1980s, crossover stars like Barbara Mandrell and Dolly Parton, who had taken giant steps beyond the confines of country music, found that their new market had only been temporary. Having lost their sense of musical direction, they also lost their larger audiences, and the recording careers of both women foundered, forcing them to return to the fold.

While crossover wasn't working, the careers of the neo-traditionalists were booming, and the money, recognition, and power they garnered was growing by leaps and bounds. "Everybody said it wouldn't work," recalls Jimmy Bowen, "but now, traditional music is the major success story in the country genre."

Dubbed "an overnight success," it had taken Reba ten long years of hard work and a grueling tour schedule to reach the top. It was a decade of experimenting and fine-tuning. "I always knew what I wanted, I just wasn't sure which way to get there." Finally, however, Reba had arrived.

A bold, newly confident Reba cut her long hair short, inspired by good buddy Barbara Mandrell. Her husband, Charlie Battles, hated the change so much he wouldn't talk to her for days.

McEntire rang in the new year by realizing one of the most important and exalted dreams of her professional life. She was asked to join the Grand Ole Opry, which she did on a highly rated CBS television special celebrating the Opry's sixtieth anniversary. (Reba became the sixty-first member.)

After performing her hit single, "Somebody Should Leave" (which always causes Reba to shed a tear or two onstage), McEntire made a moving acceptance speech, establishing her place in the Nashville music industry as a gentle-minded feminist. Reba recalled being told, early in her career, that as a woman she would find it hard to achieve success. "I heard a lot of *can'ts*—a woman can't do this and can't do that. Well, y'all just proved them wrong!" After making her inspirational speech, an always humble Reba, less impressed with her own accomplishments, ran around taking pictures backstage of her own country and western idols.

Jimmy Bowen remembers when Reba McEntire came to him, unable to figure out why she wasn't selling "really big." "I told her, 'I can make you sound great, I can get you great musicians, I can make sure your music is current, but you have to know what to say to motivate the female consumer.' " Traditionally, women have been the main

© Alan L. Mayor

Onstage, singing star Reba gets a little help from her friends.

purchasers of country (with the exception of performers like Hank Williams, Jr., who attracts the male "college rowdy crowd"), and in the past they have preferred to listen to male singers.

Pointing out to Reba that men do a "half-assed job at best" in speaking to women, Jimmy Bowen urged her to communicate with her own sex about feelings and experiences they had in common. He steered her in the direction of honesty and away from the contrived, maybe even oppressive, messages that traditional women singers were still carrying. "In this day and age, why would a woman spend money on gas, go to the record store in the mall, and fight her way through Kiss posters to get to the country section in the back, only to hear a woman singing a silly little lyric—the man is always cool! It's all so trite; say something real. I'll help you do it."

Reba replied, "I believe I can do that." Pop music had had strong women and feminist lyrics for a long while—it was time for country to play catch-up. Reba took the bull by the horns and she's been in control ever since. Taking a cue from Reba, the younger generation of female singers in Nashville has followed in her bold footsteps.

Whoever's in New England, the first of two Reba McEntire albums released in 1986, reflected her new direction. It revived the "woman-to-woman" song genre, first perfected by country greats like Kitty Wells and Tammy Wynette in the 1960s, but Reba's messages are much more modern. Usually about the men in women's lives, there are messages about sympathy, understanding, and sisterhood. Reba offers other women a shoulder to cry on, and lets them know that she's been there and knows how they feel.

The album deals mostly with heartbreak, something everyone in Reba's female (and male, for that matter) audience could relate to. "My songs are usually about everyday life," she acknowledges proudly. Whether light-hearted or sad, McEntire always voices her opinions about each experience. Family values usually triumph, and the women depicted are strong, resilient, and nonjudgmental—without any predictable or prefabricated point of view.

"Like Loretta and Tammy, I'm trying to sing songs for women—to say for them what they can't say themselves. But I'm trying to be modern in my outlook. It's not the same world it once was. Before, a lot of wives identified with 'Don't Come Home A-Drinkin with Loving on Your Mind.' Now it's, 'Don't even think about comin' home drunk because I'm not even gonna be there.' Women today are more independent. They won't take what they used to. We have to demand respect. Don't refer to me as a gal, a chick, or a broad. Women need to be strong.

My mother is one of the strongest women I've ever met in my life. She can cry right along with you at the saddest movie, but when there's trouble, she's the backbone."

Sisterhood is a continuous theme in McEntire's work. Taking a stand for women's rights, her next several albums contained "issue songs," like a rousing version of Aretha Franklin's mega-hit, "Respect" (written by a man, the late, great Otis Redding). Taking a message to women was a great responsibility, and one Reba didn't treat lightly. The subjects she tackled included sexual temptation; dealing with the feeling of being ignored by a husband who finds business or money more fascinating than his love and his wife; infidelity on both sides; and the pitfalls of having infinite freedom. "I think women are special," says Reba. "I want to make them realize that."

Bill Carter, Reba's manager at the time *Whoever's in New England* was released, confirmed why the singer was so attractive to a female audience: "Because of what Reba stands for, women enjoy a symbiotic relationship with her. They like her, so they buy her records. She has been successful in attracting the new, nineties woman—the woman who stands up for her rights."

As proof positive of Reba's influence with women, she showed up as covergirl on *Redbook,* one of the most popular of the women's magazines.

Becoming a country feminist was not a piece of cake. McEntire admits that it can be hard to impress and win over your own sex, and it takes a lot of thought. At first, she changed her stage outfits, trying not to offend her female audience, who might perceive her as crude or flirty. "I stopped wearing Spandex pants, even though they're the most comfortable britches I ever had on. I went to

She gave up wearing Spandex pants, "the most comfortable britches I ever wore," so as not to alienate female fans.

western skirts and cowgirl boots, but found I couldn't get down and sassy anymore." Realizing that superficial changes were not the answer, Reba went back to wearing the Spandex pants in a quest to avoid being phoney in any way.

"I try to be honest, not uppity, not too sexy, not trying to steal anybody's boyfriend or husband," says Reba. "I let 'em know that I've got one of my own, so let's just be friends. That way, their men can have a good time and not get into trouble for it!"

Once afraid of women, Reba now finds them her great comfort, and if she sees a lady in the audience who isn't responding to her act, she works especially hard to win her over. "I wink to let her know that we're in it together!"

GOING FOR THE GOLD 10

Whoever's in New England turned out to be the ultimate breakout record for Reba McEntire. Not only did it address the emotional side of the female experience with sensitivity, it was the only record ever to come out of Nashville with Massachusetts mentioned in the first line. A creative and savvy Reba was trying to attract new fans where country music is traditionally the least popular—the Northeast. This album also demonstrated how far Reba's amazing vocal control and power had come.

Whoever's in New England, featuring background singing by Pake McEntire, has as its cover a pensive Reba dressed in a long beige suede dress, matching cowboy boots, and her rodeo buckle, standing in front of a New England–style clapboard barn. She dedicated the record to the Road Slugs and Sluggettes—a little joke between Reba and her band, who one night, because they were late arriving at a venue, were forced to go onstage without showering.

Looking for a "career breakthrough song," the title track veered away from country's rural traditions, nudging the singer toward a more urbane audience. The song, which reached number one on the charts, examines a wife's suspicions that her husband's frequent business trips are really monkey business. With the tear-soaked voice of a woman who strives to be strong and will endure, Reba sings to the unfaithful husband. She lets him know that when the cold snow that has blinded him to the loving wife he has left behind blows away, she'll be there waiting to take him back from whoever it is that lures him to New England. One New York critic quipped that this song might start a new musical trend—"yuppie country."

"Little Rock" was the other number-one hit from the album. It's a rocking, rollicking song in which an ignored wife tells her money-obsessed husband she's going to slip off her wedding ring (the "little rock") and get herself some good loving. She'll show him that he has everything but her!

The album's opening track, "Can't Stop Now," has a woman admitting she knew what she was doing when she went into a relationship with a married man, even though she knows he makes promises he can't ever keep.

In "You Can Take the Wings Off Me," a woman who's really never been in love and is used to going home to bed alone, finally meets Mr. Right—she just wants him to be gentle with her. From happy to sad, "I'll Believe It When I Feel It" features a broken-hearted woman whose man has left her. Everybody says she'll find another man to love—he's out there waiting for her—but she doesn't believe she'll ever find him.

"I've Seen Better Days," an old Sammi Smith hit,

Courtesy of the Country Music Foundation, Inc.

Just after the release of her super-breakout album *Whoever's in New England*, Reba McEntire, with her brother, Pake, visits "Good Morning America" to discuss their family, their background in rodeo, and their singing careers. Left to right: Pake, GMA's Joan Lunden and David Hartman, Reba.

is the saddest song on the album. McEntire infuses the song, about a broken-down woman whose husband has left her and taken the kids, with a voice loaded with grief and heartache. "Sometimes," says Reba, "I get into it a little *too* much. It took me two or three times to quit crying when I recorded it. I was just movin' my lips and jaws, but nothin' was coming out because I was so choked up. Weldon Myrick was playing steel on the session, and I remember when I walked out of the sound booth, he just looked at me and said, 'You got into that a little bit, didn't you?' It's such a heart-rippin' song, I had to come back, finally, and sing it by myself."

A single, independent gal sings "If You Only Knew" to her woman friend, who's had a fight with her man and walked out on him. Reba addresses the trials and tribulations of being a single girl dealing with loneliness, waiting for the right man to love. The married woman is jealous—she wants to be free, have control, be wild. The single woman listens and is understanding, but ultimately sends her friend home where she belongs, telling her how lucky she is.

With a lot of colorful fiddling, "One Thin Dime" reveals what a no-good man who's left his woman with a broken heart needs to get back into her arms once he comes to his senses. "Don't Touch Me There" is a beautiful ballad about a woman who offers her body to a man, but not her heart—she's had it broken before, and badly, and she's scared it will happen again. "Don't Make That Same Mistake Again" is a gutsy song about a woman who's loved too much and lost, but admits she'd do it all over again.

Reba had made plans to do a music video several times before, but a video had never materialized. She was worried about not coming across well. "Sometimes, bad TV can harm you more than good TV can help you," she has said. But the material on *Whoever's in New England* was so strong that she decided to go for it. Jon Small, a New York–based director with his own company, Picture Vision, was chosen to head the effort. Reba was counting on the video for the album's title cut, shot in Boston—from the Commons to Logan Airport, right in the middle of rush-hour traffic—and in New Bedford, Massachusetts, to open the doors to new markets. And it did. More people than ever were introduced to Reba and became rabid fans.

Small, who directed the hit MTV video "Walk This Way" for rap superstars Run D.M.C. (featuring Aerosmith), had also worked with big-name pop artists like Billy Joel, Hall and Oates, John Cougar Mellencamp, and Chicago. He praised Reba's considerable natural acting talent, which was easy to bring to the surface once things got rolling on the difficult shoot. The weather was freezing, and Reba was feeling a little insecure, but she had definitely been bitten by the acting bug in a big way.

"It's not all that different from performing onstage," recalled the novice video star. "You have to go through a lot of emotions for every song."

Two weeks after wrapping production, the video premiered on "Entertainment Tonight," and more than achieved its objective. The hit song got a powerful sales boost, and the video enhanced Reba's accessibility as a performer—and occasioned an unprecedented flurry of local press activity in a town where she was the newest star attraction.

As a backup to the video, McEntire sang, danced, and chatted her way across the East Coast, charming a whole new legion of fans. "We're always trying to broaden our audience, to go somewhere we've never been before, like the Northwest—even though it's so far between towns, you eat up your profit paying for gasoline!"

Whoever's in New England was Reba McEntire's first gold album, with sales over 500,000. This was especially impressive for a woman country singer, and a harbinger of how incredibly famous she was about to become.

Riding on the coattails of the album's almost giddy success, the Academy of Country Music Awards show in April netted Reba her second consecutive "Top Female Vocalist of the Year" award from the Academy. She cohosted the two-hour NBC special with John Schneider and Mac Davis. Having done such a thoroughly professional job and proven herself as a poised TV performer, the producers of the *Music City News* Awards asked her to

It's "thumbs up" for a 1987 award from the Academy of Country Music for Reba's first gold record, *Whoever's in New England.*

do the same for them in June. At that awards show she walked away with her second consecutive "Top Female Artist" honors.

In between collecting statuettes, Reba toured extensively through California, where she was received nightly by overheated, sellout crowds who gave her a standing ovation every time out. She was in heaven!

Then it was back into the studio to record the second Reba album of the year, *What Am I Gonna*

© Kevin Winter/DMI

Clutching her statuette for "Best Female Vocalist of the Year" at the twenty-second annual Academy of Country Music Awards show in 1987, Reba looks admiringly at her second gold record.

Do About You? Released in September, just before the Country Music Awards, it went gold immediately, making it two gold albums in a row that year. The album cover, photographed at the Bidwell Mansion in Chico, California, pictures a very sedate, low-key Reba (who did her own makeup for the shoot), dressed in muted earth tones.

Once again, her brother sings background vocals on the album, and this time the liner notes contain a special message of thanks and appreciation to co-producer Jimmy Bowen as well as to the "Road Slugs" who worked with her in the studio. For her fans, she added a special message as well: "This album might not have a basic theme to it, but I hope it entertains you, relaxes you, makes you feel good, gets you to reminisce, cry and make you fall in love all over again. . . . I just hope you like our music. What am I gonna do about you? I'll tell you later. Love, Reba."

The title track, a number-one single, reminded Reba a lot of *Whoever's in New England*, so she hadn't planned to use it. But everyone around her flipped for it, so it made the cut. The song is a touching, tearful story of love lost, set to the crying of a steel pedal guitar.

The other breakout hit single from the album was "One Promise Too Late." Once again she tells a tale of love not working out, of a woman who meets Mr. Right, but only after she's already committed to another man. In the song, the woman, of course, lets her dream man go, even though it might kill her.

"My Mind Is on You," a wild song about a woman who has a lover's quarrel with her man and ends up in a bar with so many suitors it makes her head swim, was a tough choice for Reba to make. It talks about drinking margaritas and smoking cigarettes—two images Reba had always avoided before, in no small part because of the responsibility she feels to her fans to set the right example. Eventually, she decided to go with it. "Everybody liked the song," says Reba, "but I've always turned down tunes with alcohol in [them], like 'Does Fort Worth Ever Cross Your Mind?' because of the beer. I had the writers rewrite 'Today All Over Again' just to get the wine out of it. But, boy, this was such a good song, it was hard to turn down. I talked to my good buddy upstairs, the Lord, and said, 'What do you think?' After a while, I didn't feel any guilt, any pressure. It was his way of telling me to go in there and sing it."

Reba calls the opening number, "Why Not Tonight," her "Dwight Yoakum tune." In a western-swing mode, a girl—figuring it could be the start of something good, so why not—goes after a guy she's attracted to, even though she's not usually so forward. Reba thinks the song is right on target for today's modern woman.

"Lookin' for a New Love Story" is an upbeat, hopeful song, the words of a woman who has always looked upon love as a fairy tale, a dream right out of the movies. She believes that one of these days the right man will come to her and she'll star in her own love story.

A country version of a golden rock and roll oldie, "Take Me Back" opens up with some doo-wop harmony, and then rolls into a celebration of the good old days, when things were simpler, when living life in the fast lane wasn't necessarily playing with death.

"Let the Music Lift You" is a joyous salute to our national freedom and a nod to music, which relates to all of us, no matter where we live. "I Heard Her Cryin' " is an old-fashioned country song about a marital fight so ugly that it woke up the baby and made her cry. Her parents wish they could take back what they said and did, just to make their child feel safe and happy again.

In a similar musical style, but with a much different message, "No Such Thing" reminds the listener of "Harper Valley PTA"—it has the same kind of spunk. People around town gossip and say that she's got somebody new, but she's here to tell her man that there is nobody else for her and that she's true.

The final song on the album, "Till It Snows in Mexico," is a haunting ballad about everlasting love. Some people call Oklahomans old-fashioned and plain because they know the difference between wrong and right, and because when they marry it's forever. In the lyrics, she promises her husband that they belong together, that she will always love him and won't stop loving him until it snows in Mexico.

With the album finished, and still enjoying the success of her first video, Reba decided to try a second video. Nashville, New York, and Hollywood teamed up to produce a high-concept, high-budget masterpiece for the title track, "What Am I Gonna Do About You?" Shown a series of daily-life vignettes and flashbacks, the audience is never sure why this love has gone wrong. Jon Small, once again brought in to write, produce, and direct on location in New York City and Long Island, left a lot to the viewers' imagination. "There's no reason to show everything in such a concrete way," Reba observed. "It's better to let the viewers make up their own mind, relate it to their own life." The ambiguity makes it all the more accessible to a wider audience—just what Reba was hoping for.

Though it rained endlessly, the atmosphere during filming was far more relaxed than on the first video. Reba was more confident, and felt more trusting toward Small, no longer a stranger. "Our rapport was great, and in spite of the weather, there was a really good vibe." David Keith, one of the stars of *An Officer and a Gentleman*, was featured as McEntire's romantic lead. Keith, a native of Knoxville, Tennessee, had been introduced to Reba by one of her backup singers, Suzi Hoskins, at Fan Fair. He arrived just in time (via the Concorde) from working on a project in Rome, to shoot the video—a testament to his love of country music and appreciation of Reba's talents.

Working with David Keith was fun for Reba, and easy. "He makes it seem effortless because he's had so much acting experience. At times, I was having such a good time, I'd start giggling when I was supposed to be serious! It was strange to be singing in the middle of the airport—people looked at me like I was crazy. That's still the hardest part for me, shooting in crowds all alone. Like the supermarket scene: I kept looking to David for the right mood, and just followed his lead." Keith, impressed by her intensity and discipline, came to regard Reba as a natural actress.

"Emotionally, the last scene was the hardest," remembers McEntire. "We had been shooting two days. We were tired, people were fussing with my clothes and hair, and there were about twenty people crammed into one room. I'll tell you—I *felt* like crying! We had to shoot the scene three different times from three angles. I just put it into my mind that David was dead. David said he didn't want to be dead, but it's my video, and he'll die if I want him to!" Reba was so convincing there wasn't a dry eye in the house.

"Watching Reba act this time was really beautiful—like watching a flower open," observed the director. "She's improved so much."

McEntire credits her natural dramatic ability to her love of play-acting. "Every night when I perform onstage, I step into a fairy-tale world. It's not me anymore. It's that person in the song." It's easy for Reba to lose herself in fantasy, usually of the heart-rending variety, as that's what country is all about. "I get into it so much, and with my vivid imagination, it's easy to really feel sad and start crying. I try to dredge up unhappy memories from my childhood, like when Susie's puppy died, to

© Kevin Winter/DMI

. . . then she gets her hand around the golden prize. "Look, Ma, I've done it again!"

bring up those tears when I need them." Reba's audience is often so affected by her that they cry right along.

The video for "What Am I Gonna Do About You?" was a success and gave McEntire expanded visibility and exposure on HBO's "Video Jukebox," and on Showtime—in the company of top-selling contemporary singers like Aretha Franklin and Whitney Houston. The whole experience prompted a trip to Hollywood to check out acting possibilities more carefully. Even though Reba was still "pure country," she was clearly looking for fame in a larger arena.

After a year of hard work and many accolades, along came the Country Music Awards in October. An important tradition in Nashville, those who win "Entertainer of the Year" are considered to be at the zenith of their careers. The twentieth-anniversary show took place on October 13. The telecast was hosted by Kris Kristofferson and Willie Nelson; Lionel Richie performed; Ricky Skaggs sang gospel with a pre-crossover Amy Grant; and Dolly Parton, Emmylou Harris, and Linda Ronstadt introduced their new collaborative effort. Reba McEntire was nominated in five categories (tying the ultra-popular mother-daughter duo, Wynonna and Naomi Judd): "Female Vocalist of the Year," "Single," "Album," and "Video of the Year" (for "Whoever's in New England"), and the much-coveted "Entertainer of the Year." Other nominees in the final category were the Judds, Ricky Skaggs, George Strait, and Willie Nelson.

Reba, in a backless, bright blue sequin dress, was a nervous wreck all night, and almost occasioned a riot when she was awarded her third consecutive "Female Vocalist of the Year," a recognition nobody had achieved in twenty years.

All the years of hard work and struggling, the long, long effort behind becoming "an overnight sensation," were given their greatest recognition, however, when at the end of the show, Miss Reba Nell McEntire was named "Entertainer of the Year." Exclaiming, "I'm not going to cry, I'm going to faint," Reba followed with an inspirational acceptance speech, bringing the crowd to their feet. "I'm proud to carry the banner for country music. There's more and more people out there open to country, and my big ole boot will be there to kick in a door for each and every one of us."

Backstage, after the awards ceremony, she stood trembling. "I was about nearing convulsions. It's a good thing Charlie grabbed the statue—I was just about to drop it." With this final honor of the evening, Reba McEntire graduated from Princess to the Queen of Country.

At the Country Music Awards in 1986, Reba finally realizes a lifelong dream—"Entertainer of the Year."

© Alan L. Mayor

11

LIFE AFTER "ENTERTAINER OF THE YEAR"

The day after becoming CMA's "Entertainer of the Year," things seemed to be back to normal. Reba was happy that she had won, but it hadn't really changed anything. "I'm still me, and I'm still biting at the bit. I still want more, more, more and better, better, better. You know, better shows, better albums."

Slipping down to Stringtown for a little rest and relaxation, Reba was surprised by her new notoriety in the old neighborhood, where previously people had never paid her much attention when she was out shopping or at the bank. "I went to the grocery store," laughed Reba, "and shoot—there was such a commotion, I couldn't even remember what I came in there for. They were lining up for autographs, or they would just stand back and say, 'Ooh, there she is!' It was weird, and I was saying, 'C'mon y'all, I'm still just Reba. I was just in here a couple of weeks ago, and y'all didn't act like that then.' "

Finally escaping the exhaustion and elation of the limelight, Reba spent some time on the ranch

Reba presented her domestic situation as idyllic, even though it would be less than a year before she announced her divorce from Charlie Battles.

with Charlie. Once home, she pulled on her cowboy boots and headed to the barn to saddle up her quarterhorse, Leggs.

In between moving the cattle around and giving them their shots, Reba spent a good amount of time giving long-distance telephone interviews. "Yep, that's the cattle and country music business these days!" Denying that her life had anything to do with the raw, often unhappy drama found in her song lyrics, Reba presented her domestic situation as idyllic, even though it would be less than a year before she announced her divorce from Charlie Battles. Unable to resist the lure of the bright lights and applause, the trips home to Stringtown became fewer and shorter.

Even though Reba had attained one of her dreams, there was no chance that she'd rest on her laurels or slow down. Things weren't any easier for her as the leading woman in country music. There were still barriers for her to knock down, and she was getting ready to do battle. "Just after winning 'Entertainer of the Year,' someone said to me, 'Reba, now I guess women will have it easier.' I just looked at her like she was crazy and said, 'No way.' I really think it's as tough for women as it was when I started. Women still have to struggle, still have to prove themselves four times as much as any man does. The only way you're going to make it is to accept that challenge and work that much harder." Bill Carter agreed: "As hard as we've worked on Reba's career, if it had been a male artist, we'd be selling millions [of albums] more."

Still, McEntire is credited with opening the doors of Nashville for other women like the Judds, Roseanne Cash, Tanya Tucker, Crystal Gayle, Kathy Mattea, Patty Loveless, and Lorrie Morgan. Female singers were definitely considered more viable after Reba challenged the men of Music Row, demonstrating her power within the industry and before the audience. Over a three-year period in the mid-1980s, more women and women-fronted groups got Nashville record contracts than had in all the years since the '60s.

Like Janet Jackson, Reba McEntire preached control as the pathway to ultimate success. Being in charge of your own destiny and staying true to your ideals and yourself were the key. An enlightened Jimmy Bowen had been totally on the mark when he said, "Nobody knows better than Reba what's right for her."

When she started out, she had heard all the horror stories about women singers who were told to keep quiet in the studio and follow orders. "Now," insisted Reba, "I don't think there's anything I can't do."

The Reba McEntire performing machine pressed on into a new year, working toward her desire to be a household name. She was successfully wooing a new breed of fan—younger, hipper, more urban—while breaking box office records all over the nation. According to Bill Carter, "Based on our research, we figured that better than fifty percent of Reba's record buyers were non-country. We're gaining another audience. She has acted as an ambassador for country music, and helped out the whole industry. If Reba could sell records in traditionally weak markets, other artists could, too. A thirty-five-year-old woman—an engineer—came up to Reba in Detroit, saying she'd read about her in the local newspaper and had bought a cassette. The woman had never even listened to country music on the radio. This experience made me believe we can sell the world on Reba McEntire, just on the strength of her talent."

"I know a hit when I hear it—it's like a dress. You know it's right when you put it on."

At her first concert after the CMA Awards show, down in Florida, McEntire and the band went about preparing for the opening, doing everything as usual. The band went out onstage. The lights went down. The emcee went onstage. Then all of a sudden, the crowd got wilder and louder. Reba couldn't figure out what was going on. "I thought, Geez, who's out there on that stage? I figured some big star must have shown up. When I found out it was for me, I went, 'Whewee!' Right about then, the audience started stomping on the floor and chanting, 'Reba, Reba, Reba.' It freaked me out. I didn't understand it. I'm not different than I was last week."

Florida, however, was only the beginning. Everywhere she went, the crowds were almost insanely enthusiastic. Reba may not have understood the reaction, but after a while, it grew on her!

Reba made her New Year's resolutions for 1987: "I want to make it a year in country music that stands out. I'm working to improve my show and my records. My producer and I are looking for better songs—a better blend. In truth, her resolve was set quite some time before 1987. McEntire seemed to have an unerring ability to pick, write, and record the hit songs. "I know a hit when I hear it—it's like a dress. You know it's right when you put it on. A good song will affect you emotionally. You have to imagine yourself in the same situation, and see if it works."

In order to make her stage appearance seamless, each of her performances was videotaped for review later. That way Reba could iron out any snags. "We'll take out what's not good and add what's better, though you never want to be too slick. Perfection is not entertaining. When I'm onstage, all my energy, tension, and emotions go into the show. I give it all I've got."

Keeping up her high-profile journey into mainstream stardom, Reba and her band were doing an exhausting 270 days a year on the road, "trying never to sing a song the same way twice." They traveled from city to city in a caravan of two customized Silver Eagle tour buses, followed by a pickup truck loaded with equipment.

Most of Reba's private time was confined to a compartment in the back of her bus outfitted with a wide bunk bed, makeup mirror, stained glass windows, and lavender bathroom. Being a star might seem glamorous, but Reba's grueling tour schedule often left her on the brink of exhaustion and lonely for some home life. Being a trouper, though, she pressed on. "It's the touring that keeps the money coming in," she noted—so she could pay her staff of eleven, all with families to feed.

12 D-I-V-O-R-C-E

Nineteen eighty-seven was a year of milestones for Reba Nell McEntire, some of them joyous, some of them sad. For months before she went into the studio in January to cut a new album, *The Last One to Know*, there had been rumors swirling about the state of Reba's marriage to Charlie Battles. In spite of denials and protestations, her next record—filled with sadness, anger, and marital strife—fueled the fire. Though she seemed like the girl with everything, Reba was going through some dark moments.

Like the famous Tammy Wynette album *D-I-V-O-R-C-E*, *The Last One to Know* was a somber and generally downbeat group of compositions, most of them written by women (including Reba herself). Many critics, calling the latest effort a concept album, had chafed at the predictability of McEntire's last several records. This one, about the disintegration of marriage from the wife's point of view, was more substantial. And it did offer a few hopeful possibilities regarding the achievement of marital bliss.

The big question on everybody's mind was how much of the material on the album was autobiographical. Of course, only Reba could know for sure, but she was much too private a person and too respectful of the feelings of others to talk openly of her marital problems. There's no question, however, that *The Last One to Know* was full of songs from the heart. Even the cover of the album, featuring a dejected, sad-looking Reba in casual clothes in an obviously western setting, made the album seem especially personal.

An important record for many reasons, *The Last One to Know* was, in a sense, for many years McEntire's only public comment on her split with Charlie Battles. It turned out to be Reba's third consecutive gold record, and contained two hit singles—the title track and "Love Will Find Its Way to You." Not bad, as one record reviewer commented, "for someone who still needs two syllables to pronounce *lips*!"

The title track has a wife looking back at a failed marriage. She doesn't understand how she didn't notice that her marriage, which once burned like fire, had turned to ashes. She laments that she should have felt it, or seen it in her husband's eyes. Instead, she had clung to her belief that he would never leave her, so when he said goodbye and left, it was a shattering experience. Reba sings the lyrics with depth and passion, plus a little bitterness.

The theme of marital discord continues on the album with "The Girl Who Has Everything." The most striking song of the group, it tells the story of an ex-wife buying a present for her former husband's new bride. "I Don't Want to Mention Any

With Charlie Battles in happier times.

Names" is a honky-tonk number about a wife confronting the woman who's trying to steal her man. The wife has noticed the little hussy coming on to her husband, and she's determined to fight to the death to keep him. "Someone Else" is meant to soothe a jealous husband who thinks his wife is cheating on him. With a strong and confident voice, she tells him it's all in his mind—her love is here to stay.

A husband and wife who are divorcing are busy splitting up their possessions in "What You Gonna Do About Me?" While they're dividing up the TV, the dishes, the cars, and records, their small daughter wants to know what's going to happen to her.

Reba revealed her social consciousness with "Just Across the Rio Grande," a somewhat unusual message song, and slightly out of keeping with the other songs in the album. The lyrics tell of an impoverished Mexican man with a wife and child (and another on the way) who stares across the Rio Grande at the lights of Laredo. He's dreaming of the world there, where people eat three meals a day. He has no money and no food and no job, and curses the bleakness of his family's future. The Rio Grande is not a big river—a boy could throw a stone across its muddy waters and hit the opposite bank—but for the Mexican man, the other side is a world away.

"I Don't Want to Be Alone," a Reba McEntire composition, has a single woman trying to tell a man she's interested in him. Afraid of dying of embarrassment (it's happened to her before), she begs him to meet her halfway. It's a simple song, with direct, expressive lyrics, and interesting enough to make Reba's fans wish she would try her hand at more songwriting.

"The Stairs," by far the most disturbing song on the album, is a plaintive waltz, a song about a marriage turned violent. A battered wife is confused, angry, and frustrated by her husband's abuse, but doesn't know what to do. She wants to leave, but is afraid. To explain the bruises that are inflicted when he hits her, she tells everyone she fell down the stairs. He promises each time it won't happen ever again, but it always does. Reba included this song to send a message to abused women. Many of Reba's fans were convinced that the song was about the singer's own marital experiences, were sure she had suffered some form of physical or mental abuse at Charlie's hand, though Reba has always denied this.

"Love Will Find Its Way to You" carries an inspirational message to those who haven't found love.

Charlie was criticized in the press for being a "one-man metaphor for chauvinism," and many people assumed he was abusing Reba.

Keep your hope up, the lyrics say, and let your natural attributes shine through. Show your true feelings to the world, keep believing, and Mr. Right will find you. As a poignant final cut, "I've Still Got the Love We Made" underscores that even though the marriage is over and the mementos might be gone, she will have memories of a love that was once wonderful for the rest of her life. It brings the marriage full circle, and ends the album with the message that time will heal all wounds.

This album caused alarm among some of Reba's devoted fans, who were concerned about the emotional, physical, and marital state of their singing idol. Charlie was criticized in the press for being a "one-man metaphor for chauvinism," and many people assumed he was abusing Reba. For others, *The Last One to Know* really struck a nerve, since many of them were going through a similar situation and could relate to the messages of sadness tempered with hope that the songs offered.

Reba McEntire is from a religious background, however, and many of her most devoted fans are religious folk as well. Some of these people adhere to the strict belief that marriage is a sacred bond never to be broken, no matter what the cost. Obviously Reba had progressed beyond these fundamentalist beliefs. Still, it must have been a painful, wrenching time for her, full of self-doubt and concern for what her fans might think.

Reba did not address her marital situation in public, but she did file for divorce from Battles in Atoka, Oklahoma, on June 25, 1987. She cited irreconcilable differences arising in the eleven-year marriage, but refused to comment on those in public.

A year later, Reba looked back at her situation then. "It wasn't easy getting divorced. I had to pack up and leave in one day. It was totally starting over—I didn't even have a bed." While she couldn't come out and say what was wrong with the marriage or what caused it finally to break up, people around her couldn't help notice the bitterness she obviously felt toward her ex-husband.

Just after Reba remarried, she offered a bit more explanation about the bust-up with Battles, though her words still had an angry edge. "We had our differences, our ups and downs like any other marriage. I guess things really started to go wrong when I made 'Entertainer of the Year.' Charlie thought it was time for me to slow down, when I was thinking things were just beginning. I was in love, and the next day, I was out of love."

After divorcing Charlie Battles, Reba never had any further contact with him or his two sons, referring to the marriage as her past life. "When things are over for me—they are over."

Some of Reba's fans did react badly to her breakup. She had always presented her marriage in public as solid as a rock, and it shocked people that a sweet, family-oriented girl like "just plain Reba" (as she likes to call herself) was involved in something as tawdry as divorce. Letters denouncing her split stacked up. Reba was deeply hurt by the backlash, but made an effort to answer everyone who had written to her. "I was sincere, and told them it was my business, and they'd just have to trust me. One woman said my songs were the reason she stayed with her husband. I told her not to do it because of me. Another said, 'How dare you? I've had you on a pedestal for years and now you've ruined my life.' I told her to get her eyes off me and focus them on God." Eventually the furor died down, and ultimately this emotional ordeal

"I was sincere, and told them it was my business, and they'd just have to trust me. One woman said my songs were the reason she stayed with her husband. I told her not to do it because of me."

strengthened Reba's appeal to women as a strong role model.

After divorce proceedings were concluded, Reba named her former steel pedal guitar player and road manager, Narvel Blackstock, as her business manager—a position Charlie Battles had held for some time. Married since the age of sixteen and the father of three children, Blackstock was going through his own divorce around the same time, in Texas. Later Blackstock would become Reba's husband. After the split from Charlie, Reba was questioned about the possibility of remarrying—it was rumored that she was already in love. "I told God, 'I'm not pickin' the next one; you are!' Things just didn't work out the first time. I want the next man to be right. No more mistakes."

Rather than dwell on the unhappiness of her divorce, Reba did double duty in the studio, recording her Christmas album at the same time she was working on *The Last One to Know.* McEntire was afraid she was flooding the market with too much material, especially since her *Greatest Hits* album was due out that year as well. Jimmy Bowen forced the issue and once again proved to have the right formula for success.

At the Grammys in February, Reba won "Best Country Vocal Performance/Female." It was an honor, but something happened that momentarily ruined the night for her. Backstage, she went up to notoriously rude pop star Sting, stuck out her hand, and introduced herself. "He didn't even acknowledge my existence," said an obviously hurt Reba. "I was so embarrassed; I never felt so small in my life." The snub only made her more determined that everybody would come to know who she was.

But the night was not a total loss. Reba was impressed with the professional camaraderie and how much singers from different genres all had in common. "Musically, things have opened up for all of us—we're singers, no matter what our style. I was backstage, having a nice chat with Carl Perkins, Huey Lewis, Roger Miller, and Kim Carnes. It was fun getting to meet people from different parts of the music world, like Run D.M.C.—I'd heard their music, but it was a real kick to talk to them in person."

The Grammy was followed by two American Country Music Awards in the early spring—"Top Female Vocalist" and "Video of the Year" for "Whoever's in New England." Onstage that night, Reba's performance was the highlight of the show. Standing alone in the spotlight on an otherwise empty stage, McEntire awed the crowd (and the TV audience) with the vocal range, perfect pitch, and clarity she brought to bear in an a capella version of Patsy Cline's "Sweet Dreams." Her performance—and the response to it—was proof that country music can be vastly appealing without any dilution. While her country accent and inflection were constant, her voice was "almost operatic in its emotional force and precision," one critic noted.

Bill Carter recalled, "When we talked about Reba doing the song, the director of the show said, 'It's never been done before. How will you [Reba] be able to keep your timing and your pitch? It's very risky, but if you want to take a chance, it's your career.' Needless to say, it was a huge success!"

Fan Fair, in June, was a mob scene. Reba-lovers lined up seemingly for miles to get close to "just plain Reba," the redhead with a great set of pipes who brought glitz and glitter to the circus atmosphere.

One for each hand! Reba scores big at the American Music Awards.

© Kevin Winter/DMI

In an embarrassment of riches, the awards and kudos kept piling up (Reba would earn a record-setting eight from various organizations by year's end). NARM named *Whoever's in New England* as "Best Selling Country Album by a Female." From *Music City News*, Reba received "Female Artist of the Year," and they awarded her as well for "Country Music Video of the Year." Reba was truly overwhelmed and gratified. "I never take any of these awards for granted. We're all human and we all want attention."

After announcing her divorce, Reba did something radical but long overdue—she moved to Nashville. It was, after all, already her city. "Moving was a tough decision," she's said. "I think it upset my mama more than anyone. I'm very close to her, and she didn't want me so far away. It was the logical thing to do, though, since my business is here."

When October rolled around, it was obvious to everyone that Reba McEntire had climbed to the top of country's Mount Olympus—she won a fourth consecutive "Female Vocalist of the Year" award from the Country Music Association—an accomplishment no country star, man or woman, has ever duplicated. Reba was happy she'd followed her heart and taken over the direction of her own career. Her lack of ego and continual striving for improvement gave her a unique charm. "The more successful I become, the harder I work. I want to do more videos, restage my live show, and stay ahead of the game. When we go gold, I'm already thinking about platinum. I want to sell out bigger halls."

13 HOWDY, CARNEGIE HALL

Near the end of summer, Reba went on a swing through California and the Midwest with her razzle-dazzle stage show, wowing the crowds wherever she went. Then she proceeded on to the Northeast, traditionally the toughest market for country music. Having already won over New Englanders with her 1986 hit album, Reba was intent on proving the region full of potential Reba and country fans.

"Everybody in Boston was coming up to me, telling me how proud they were when *Whoever's in New England* came out. I don't know who started the rumor that nobody likes country music up here, but I'd like to stop it quick. They're definitely wrong. We've played New Jersey, Long Island, Massachusetts, Vermont, and Maine—and all of the shows have been sellouts. I can't believe the enthusiasm of the audiences—some of the fans are following us from state to state."

Next stop—"Howdy, Carnegie Hall!" For Reba Nell McEntire, her gig at Carnegie Hall was surely

Courtesy of the Country Music Foundation, Inc.

Good old country comes to the Big Apple—the Lone Star Cafe, June 1982.

one of the most electrifying and important shows of her career, and a glorious way to end one of the most unsettling years of her private life. Before arriving in New York City, a place she'd played once before and visited several times, Reba attended "A Taste of Oklahoma" dinner in Washington, D.C. Hosted by Oklahoma Senators Don Nickels and David Boren, Governor Henry Bellmon, and members of the state's congressional delegation, it was a welcome taste of back-home.

Then, she proceeded on to Carnegie Hall, a sophisticated, urban, and hard-to-please venue not known for its love of country music. In fact, the last country singers to play Carnegie Hall had been Loretta Lynn and Buck Owens in the 1960s.

The history and legacy of this famous temple to High Culture couldn't help but daunt McEntire, whose previous appearance in New York City had been in 1982 at the Lone Star Cafe, a tiny downtown bar on Manhattan's Thirteenth Street and Fifth Avenue, a hip but unsophisticated showplace featuring killer chili on its menu and a giant iguana on the roof.

It was almost unheard of for a performer of any kind to go directly to Carnegie Hall without testing the waters at similar places first. "There was a lot of risk in coming here," observed Bill Carter. "A lot of people in Nashville and a lot of people in New York warned me not to try a concert at Carnegie Hall. We deliberately didn't play the city for the last five years. We felt when we came in, we wanted it to be a prestige event."

The week before the concert, Reba was vigorously pursued by the New York media. She had lots of TV and radio coverage, including an appearance on the "Today Show," where Jane Pauley confessed admiration for the singer.

A weak-kneed Reba approached her Carnegie Hall debut nervously. "New Yorkers are different," she explained. "They're used to sophisticated entertainment." She had nothing to worry about, however—the show was a sellout. A momentarily fragile Reba recalls, "I took in the crowd and their enthusiasm, and I almost started crying. But then I thought, Now I got a show to do."

It was a fast-paced, controlled, but not too-slick show that stressed simple emotion both directly and deeply. Reba opened with a lively rendition of the jingoistic "Let the Music Lift You Up." The audience came alive, and stayed that way for the rest of the evening.

The show featured a mix of old-style ballads like "What Am I Gonna Do About You?" with modern-woman anthems, "Lookin' for a New Love Story."

Good old country tunes were interspersed with torchy numbers. The standard "Since I Fell for You" went over so well that it made it onto her next album. Reba's vocal chops, reminiscent of "a rodeo version of Lena Horne," according to one critic, won over the tough New York audience, impressed with a kind of confidence possessed by very few performers.

After the encore, a gorgeous version of "Sweet Dreams," the crowd erupted into thunderous applause, offering up a five-minute standing ovation to the elated star—an "irresistible bundle of grits and glitz." Critics and industry types were stunned. Said one, "Nobody gets a standing ovation in New York. Not in pop, not in rock, and certainly not in country. Not even the Pope gets one here."

Ron Delsner, the well-known music promoter who handled the Carnegie Hall date, pronounced the evening an unqualified success. "New York is a very hard market, especially for this kind of music," he said. "Judging from what happened here, Reba obviously has a crossover audience. She's a great vocalist with incredible range—her voice is one of the more impressive instruments in any kind of popular music. I want to bring her back."

Bill Carter agreed that Reba's appearance at Carnegie Hall was "the most significant move we've made in her career. Not everyone can or should play it, but Reba is such a powerful vocalist and a poised performer, it was an obvious choice."

Triumphant and exhausted, Reba herself said it had been a thrill. With a little wink, she added, "We did okay, didn't we? Whew."

After making her mark on the Big Apple, Reba headed to Oklahoma for a tour and a visit with her

© Beth Gwinn/Retna Ltd.

Reba blew the audience away at her triumphal appearance at Carnegie Hall in 1987. She was the first country act to play there in almost twenty years.

© Beth Gwinn/Retna Ltd.

Reba loves the holiday season so much that she put out *Merry Christmas to You*, full of songs and some old-fashioned storytelling.

family. As if she needed any more good news, *Reba McEntire's Greatest Hits* became her first platinum record, with sales topping 1,000,000. The disc contained everybody's favorite Reba tunes: "Just a Little Love," "He Broke Your Memory Last Night," "How Blue," "Somebody Should Leave," "Have I Got a Deal for You," "Only in My Mind," "Whoever's in New England," "Little Rock," "What Am I Gonna Do About You," and "One Promise Too Late." The years of collaboration with Jimmy Bowen had been nothing short of a golden age of sheer genius. Reba McEntire had come a long way since "I Don't Want to Be a One Night Stand."

Going platinum was a lifelong dream fulfilled—Reba had worked steadily to make it happen. Once, however, was never enough for her. She was already making big plans for her next platinum success.

Still reeling from the drama and excitement of the past year, Reba appeared on "Bob Hope's Christmas Special" on December 19. Since then, she has been asked back every year—Hope loves working with her.

Issued late that year, McEntire's holiday record, *Merry Christmas to You*, contained a personal message to each and every fan: "There's a special feeling that goes with Christmas. I've got it and we hope you feel it, too!" Offered as a "piece of Reba of your very own," the album featured brand-new arrangements of seasonal favorites like "Away in the Manger," "O Holy Night," "Silent Night," "White Christmas," "I'll Be Home for Christmas," and "Happy Birthday Jesus." On the album, Reba also did some storytelling with "The Christmas Guest," a tale for kids of all ages.

14 A NEW DIRECTION

In a career where the only constant had been change, Reba sensed her audience was again ready for something new. Making an abrupt about-face from her neo-traditionalist leanings, McEntire's new album, *Reba*, was a sharp contrast to her last several albums.

The album showed her slipping into a more mainstream pop style, with a little r & b, gospel, and torch thrown in—just what she had rejected earlier in her career. With traditional country music booming, it seemed odd timing for Reba now to seek crossover fame. Her hardcore country fans found the switch shocking and accused her of selling out. A profile of country music that ran in *The New Yorker* when the album came out discussed McEntire's defection from the straight and narrow path of country purists. "Journeyman careerists like Reba McEntire are restricted. They are assured of being welcome as long as they don't break any of country's rules—it's a genre that loves its history too well."

Reba defended her choice of material. She had no intention of abandoning country music; this was a move to branch out, grow, seek another challenge—her favorite thing. The new material, "on the edge of country, on the edge of pop," was merely a reflection of her changing life. The past twelve months had seen her go from married Okie cowgirl to a single, independent Nashville superstar and accomplished businesswoman. "Come on," said the sprightly redhead to her critics, "listen to the way I talk. I'm not leaving country or turning my back on my roots. I'm looking for ten monster songs, no matter what category they fit into. The country music file has such a broad spectrum, from traditional to bluegrass to pop—there's a lot of freedom."

Reba is a very glossy record. Even the cover photo of the star shines with sophistication. Gone from the songs are the steel pedal guitar and the fiddles. Instead, the record features smooth string arrangements and background vocals, and the production values are seamless. Reba's voice is as pure and clear as ever, and the songs still focus on relationships between men and women. Unlike in her earlier, more robustly country albums, emotional ups and downs are communicated in a more subtle, gentler, sophisticated manner—although Reba's singing continues to be powerful and expressive.

Though the decision to go in a pop direction was controversial, Reba hadn't failed to notice that crossover fame, when it worked, meant big money and mass-market audiences. "With *Whoever's in New England,* where we turned a little bit more pop," explained McEntire, "my albums started turning gold. It's evident we found the right direction—it's the one I'll keep."

These days, Reba performs all kinds of music—pure country, torch, pop, even gospel. "I love it all!"

A formal Reba shoots the breeze with record executive Al Teller.

Not everybody agreed with Reba, and there were plenty of hate letters from hardcore country purists, but she was determined to stretch her repertoire and defied any pigeonholing of her talent. "In the early eighties, I was singing songs that were contemporary country, and I wanted to do something different. Nowadays, when everyone else is so traditionally minded, I want to change again; I don't want to be like everybody else. Put me in a category and I'll bust out. I'm a redhead!"

Instead of sabotaging her career, Reba McEntire once again proved her judgment was right on the mark. *Reba*, a calculated risk, had a happy ending: It was certified gold soon after release. "I want the audience to wonder what Reba McEntire will be up to tonight. When I get predictable, that's when I have to do something new; otherwise I get stale. My momma said that when I was born, my attention span was zilch. It's just gone downhill from there!"

On the set of the "Sunday Kind of Love" video, director Jack Cole offers advice to the neophyte actress.

The first cut, "So, So, So Long," is a joyous celebration of lasting love. It tells of a man and a woman who have been together for so long, and have been so close, that they know each other as intimately as two people can. It's a perfect relationship, and both are looking forward to years more of true happiness. Certainly this opening cut from the album is a far cry from anything heard on *The Last One to Know*, her previous original compilation. Apparently Reba was not only changing her style, she was changing her outlook as well.

"Sunday Kind of Love," a jazzy Etta James classic, cowritten by Louis Prima, became a Top Five

Elegance and sophistication from a bygone era—the stage set for the "Sunday Kind of Love" video.

© Alan L. Mayor

© Alan L. Mayor

Movie and television star Lou Gossett, filming *Roots Christmas*, visits Reba on the set of "Sunday Kind of Love."

© Alan L. Mayor

Dressed in 1940s torch style, Reba sings her heart out for the "Sunday Kind of Love" video.

hit for McEntire. It's another song about enduring love—more than love at first sight, more than a weekend fling. Reba performed the song on "Hour Magazine" and on "Bob Hope's NBC Birthday Special." As she explained, "We wanted to do a torch song after the success with 'Since I Fell for You' at Carnegie Hall—the critics just went nuts about it."

"New Fool at an Old Game" is a hopeful tune about new love and the shyness that goes with it. "You're the One I Dream About" tells of a woman involved in an extramarital affair. She has to keep her true love secret from the world, but can't stop dreaming of the man she really loves.

There was speculation that the sentimental ballad "Silly Me" may have mirrored Reba's feelings about her new romance with Narvel Blackstock. The song's lyrics are about two friends who fall for each other, with the woman abandoning caution and giving in to love, even though she's been hurt before.

On "Respect" Reba rocks through her own version of the Otis Redding classic (made famous by Aretha Franklin), with a lot of spunk and tons of vibrato, accompanied by some mean electric guitar. A wild choice to be sure, but Reba does it justice. She performed the song live on "The Arsenio Hall Show" and at the annual Country Music Association Awards show. "I did the song because I figured all the women out there would like it, and they did!"

Not all the tunes on *Reba* go against the country grain. "Do Right by Me" is a more traditional song of the pain of love. Likewise, "I Know How He Feels" is a woman's lament over a love gone sour. Unlike some of the no-good, cheating men on other Reba McEntire albums, however, this one is blameless for the breakup—it wasn't his fault things went wrong, it was just life.

"Wish I Were Only Lonely" is about a single girl who could stand being alone, if only she weren't lonely for that special man, the one who's not around anymore. "Everytime You Touch Her" is a sad, angry song directed at an old lover, the lyric backed by a haunting acoustic guitar.

The album, while different from what fans were expecting, was every bit as bold and affecting as Reba's more directly country-flavored efforts. "I want versatility in my music, although you're running a risk when you're in a certain category and you veer into something different. I love my fans. I wouldn't be here if it weren't for them. But I need excitement, or my music won't have feeling anymore."

Rock and roll Reba shocks and delights her audience with a new stage show and costumes worthy of any pop star.

At the epicenter of "the pop controversy," Reba McEntire went on a Hollywood-style glamour binge, adding flashing lights, colored smoke, and a huge, eye-catching set to her stage shows. Her blue jeans vanished, along with the famous Reba rodeo buckle, replaced by several glitzy, spangled costume changes per show, with lots of black leather and fashionably clad backup singers—what one might see at a rock concert, trendy nightclub, or even in Las Vegas.

McEntire said she made the changes for her fans, to make sure their night with her would be memorable. "I've come to the conclusion that if all you see at a concert is somebody up there with cowboy boots and a guitar, you may as well buy the album and stay home. When I go to a live show, I want to see spectacle, and so do other people." It was a well-thought-out plan, and it worked as expected. Suddenly, Reba could fill an 8,000-seat concert hall with no problem. She was having a great time, enjoying her success, and she had every intention of pushing it as far as she could go.

A black leather–clad Reba does an abrupt about-face, going in a more mainstream pop direction, boosting her popularity even more.

Nineteen eighty-eight ended Reba's four-year run as "Female Vocalist of the Year" at the Country Music Association Awards show, which she co-hosted with Randy Travis. Speaking to the press with predictable, homespun candor, Reba agreed that winning was better than losing, but she was extremely gracious to the new winner, K. T. Oslin. The tabloids featured a feud between the two women, interpreting an innocent statement by K. T. at the ceremony—"It's been a hell of a run, Reba!"—as sniping.

"I'm the old has-been here," Reba joked backstage. "I love being nominated, but after you've

© Kevin Winter/DMI

Yet another award for the glamorous Reba McEntire from the Academy of Country Music at Universal Studios in Hollywood.

RIGHT

Wearing a "fancy" spangled dress and sporting a big Nashville hairdo, Reba makes an appearance at the American Music Awards in Hollywood.

© Kevin Winter/DMI

LEFT

Nowadays superstar Reba always goes for the glamour.

won so many awards, it's time for somebody else to win. You don't want to ride a good horse to death. I'm glad K. T. won—I really appreciate her. She's spunky and brought something different to country music we all needed."

The year was hardly without its honors for the superstar. Reba was named "Top Female Vocalist" at the American Music Awards (for the fourth time in a row), by the *Music City News*, and at the TNN Viewers' Choice Awards. Her home state honored Reba as "Oklahoman of the Year," while the annual *People* Magazine Poll listed McEntire as their readers' next-to-favorite female singer—just behind her own teenage idol, Barbra Streisand, and out in front of Cher and Madonna.

The Gallup Youth Survey announced that American teenagers had picked Reba as one of their top ten female vocalists (no other country stars made the list), ranking her above Cyndi Lauper, Pat Benatar, and Stevie Nicks. "It wasn't a surprise," says Reba, "because we see [teenagers] at our concerts, wearing George Michael and Def Leppard t-shirts. Sometimes they come in with their parents, frowning, like they don't want to be there. After the show, they'll come up and say, 'I don't like country music, but I like you.' I'm just tickled pink about it. Liking country is suddenly hip. The younger generation will be our audience for the next ten years. They can relate to what I sing about—it's something that happens to them every day."

15 NASHVILLE YOUTHQUAKE

As the 1980s came to an end, it was possible for stars like Reba McEntire, Garth Brooks, and Allan Jackson to sell millions and millions of records, tapes, and compact discs because they were not only appealing to traditionally non-country fans, but had also managed to grab the attention of the younger generation. Babyboomers, now approaching middle age, had grown up on the popular music of the '60s and '70s, songs with strong and meaningful messages. "The lyrics were killer then," says Jimmy Bowen, now at the helm of Capitol Nashville. "You give them lyric music again, with messages they can relate to, and they'll buy it."

Young people are constantly pushing buttons on their radio dials these days, looking for and listening to a wide range of music. If they're not from the inner city, they probably can't relate to rap, even if they like it. When they come across a song like Garth Brooks' "Friends in Low Places," it's something that's going to speak to them—a song that mirrors the kind of world they all live in. "For the first time in twenty-five years," says Bowen, "there are young people in country music—and youth attracts youth. Once you've let the young people into the business, it's theirs."

With younger artists, younger lyrics, and a widespread, ever-expanding audience, country music is growing at an unbelievable rate, and it's competitive with the other music forms. Also, the definition of country music covers a lot more territory nowadays, when almost anything goes.

"Unlike pop or rock music, with high costs for everything, it's a lot easier to make a profit in Nashville, and that makes it an attractive place to work," explains Jimmy Bowen. The possibilities for enormous success are there for the taking. And Reba, who helped bring country music to its exalted state, was first in line to push it as far as it could go, looking for new levels of popularity and acceptance. Her new fans were coming from everywhere; not only had aging baby-boomers discovered her exciting sound, but suddenly she was a teen fave as well.

But every now and then, celebrity has its pitfalls, even for someone who enjoys it as much as Reba McEntire. "It's nice to be popular, but it gets frustrating when I want to go out and have a good time. I'll always sign an autograph, even if it isn't the best situation, because I'd never embarrass a fan of mine." Reba is devoted to her fans because they've elevated her to the position of High Priestess of Nashville, and Reba never forgets how she got there. After every live show, McEntire always invites members of her fan club to a backstage reception, where she is very much in evidence, sincere and friendly. During a recent Fan Fair week, she even went so far as to honor her adoring legions by throwing them a Rockin' '50s dance party.

An uncontrollable fan herself when it comes to certain legendary people, Reba got to meet one of her all-time idols, Jimmy Stewart, while appearing with him and Charlton Heston on a Bob Hope show. She was in her dressing room, hair in curlers, when somebody told her Stewart was in the building. "I yelled, 'Quick! Grab the camera!' I walked right up to him and introduced myself, and he was as nice as he could be," Reba recalls.

While working on Hope's "Drug Free America" campaign, she also got a chance to meet with then–First Lady Nancy Reagan, and filmed a "Just Say No to Drugs" spot as a public service. Reba's message encouraged kids to keep the lines of communication to their parents open.

By the beginning of 1989, Reba had won so many honors, accolades, and trophies that she often

Backstage at the 1988 Country Music Association Awards with Tony Graham.

© Alan L. Mayor

joked she'd have to buy a building just to keep all her prizes in one place. Then she did just that. In a move to take total control over her entire creative and financial empire, Reba McEntire became chairman of her own corporation, Starstruck.

The first step was severing her ties with manager Bill Carter. Then Reba bought an extensive, modern two-story corporate complex in West Nashville, just a few miles from Music Row. Naming Narvel Blackstock as her cochairman of the board, McEntire, who had already emerged as the consummate performer, proved to be just as savvy at business. Employing forty people, Reba, from her sprawling office, oversees an organization set up to handle her bookings, publicity, fan club, publishing interests, promotion, accounting, and ticket sales. In an effort to expand even further, Narvel has also begun to manage other artists.

Reba's business setup is similar to in-house concert divisions developed by other country superstars like Randy Travis, the Judds, and legendary old-timers the Statler Brothers. The greatest benefit of the arrangement is that it allows Reba to have total control over every aspect of her show's promotion and staging. In other words, she's in the best possible position to make sure she gets what she wants and needs to keep her going strong.

"Starting Starstruck meant more expenses, a bigger payroll, and having to work more dates to pay these people, but it's also made my career a lot more thought out. It was a big challenge, but I said, 'Why not? Let's go for it.' " For Reba, the biggest personal benefit by far is the excellent communication she enjoys with her staff, a bunch of "bright, hungry, dedicated people heading up every department." Proclaims a satisfied Reba, "I'm totally taken care of!"

The winner of so many awards, McEntire had to buy a whole building in Nashville to display them!

© Beth Gwinn/Retna Ltd.

Starstruck, in 1992, is a different place than it was in 1989. As with Reba's career, the whole operation has grown and become more sophisticated. "When I first bought this place, it was like a big warehouse. Now it's been converted to office space, songwriting rooms, even our own recording studio for demo records." Her aggressive, hands-on approach to life and music has paid off, disproving the theory that you can't hire your friends and family and thrive.

In an office filled with gold and platinum records and awards, everybody agrees that Reba has stayed humble. It's that quality that keeps her fans loyal. Also, she's more secure about her talent and her ability to call the shots, and for a person who spent so much of her life trying so hard to please, it's a relief to find it has all worked out. "My aim is to stay happy and keep growing. And to keep entertaining—as long as the connection with the audience survives—and I can deliver a quality show."

16 WEDDING BELLS

Making her annual trip into the studio, Reba (famous enough to be identified on albums from now on by her first name only) recorded one of the best records of her career. Reflecting her newfound romantic happiness, the record is upbeat, hopeful, and downright joyous. McEntire's fans were thrilled for her personally, and happy to see her back in the fold.

Compared to her last record—*Reba*—*Sweet Sixteen* has a real country influence. Fellow country artists Vince Gill, Steve Wariner, and Patty Loveless sing background harmony, and making a return appearance on many of the cuts are the steel pedal guitar, fiddles, and dobros. On the cover, Reba is dressed in a fashionable black outfit trimmed with tan suede. And if some of the country was still missing from her music, the country influence sure wasn't missing in her big Nashville hairdo!

Once again Reba included in the album notes her usual message to her devoted audience: "When I look back, as far as 1977 to my earlier albums, I start to relate my music to growing up. With my first LP, I was a baby, and then with each album the growth is there just like a child going through grade school and junior high school. Some show a little change, a little rebellion, but mostly they show me how much I've learned in the last fifteen albums. Now I'm a teenager with this new album. I'm 'Sweet Sixteen' all over again! That means I've got a lot to learn on down the road to finish my education."

This sixteenth album of Reba's career really shows her versatile talent as a songwriter—she coauthored three of the ten songs. The first cut on the record is an old Everly Brothers hit, "Cathy's Clown." Reba slowed the tempo down, however, giving the song a western flair and adding emphasis to the song's lyrics. It's a tale of a man so in love with Cathy that he'll do almost anything to keep her, but she doesn't love him and just makes fun of him. He won't let go; Reba, like a helpful friend, sounds as if she's really sorry for him, but he ought to stop worrying about being Cathy's clown and start thinking about being "Reba's king!" With more outlets than ever for music videos, McEntire took advantage of the media to "match the face, the name, and the song," shooting a music video with TV star Bruce Boxleitner ("Scarecrow and Mrs. King") for "Cathy's Clown."

" 'Til Love Comes Again" is a waltz featuring some killer fiddling. A woman is waiting and hoping for love to come to her again. Sometimes she's sad and memories of unhappy love affairs haunt her, but she's going to be strong until she's found the right man for her. In a collaborative effort with Kandal Franceschi and Quentin Powers (the songwriters of "Whoever's in New England"), Reba wrote "It Always Rains on Saturday," a sad song,

© Alan L. Mayor

At the TNN Viewers' Choice Awards, Reba accepts honors for *Sweet Sixteen*, everybody's favorite album.

dripping with emotion, about a love lost and lonesome weekends when her child goes to visit her ex-husband.

Another McEntire songwriting collaboration is "Am I the Only One Who Cares." It's a twangy tune that would be right at home at a square dance, and features a lyric reflecting the album title, all about a teenage girl who has a fight with her mama. She locks herself in her room, crying that nobody understands her. Ultimately, she realizes that her mother really does love her and cares about what happens to her, even if they don't always agree.

"Somebody Up There Likes Me" is a swinging pop-gospel number featuring some refreshing saxophone riffs. Yet another song Reba wrote (with Don Schlitz), "You Must Really Love Me" allows her to express both disbelief and relief that she's found love after so much disappointment. Obviously reflecting her own newfound happiness and true love, Reba tells her man that he must really love her, inasmuch as he puts up with the crazy things she says and does.

"Say the Word" is a wonderful love song with elegant harmonies. With just a dash of heartbreak thrown in for good measure, "Little Girl" has a woman recalling her childhood—her father, puppy dogs, a house with a picket fence, the ice cream man. She has spent her life chasing after things she wants, but now she's made a mistake in chasing after a man who doesn't want her, and it hurts.

With "Walk On," the long-lasting hit single, Reba flexes her vocal cords and delivers an inspirational message of steely determination to keep on going when things get you down. Bad times won't last forever if you just keep pushing on. This composition could be Reba's own personal anthem. She belts out "A New Love"—about the joys and fear of falling in love. A burgeoning relationship might not turn out to be perfect, but it's the best way of assuring yourself that you're alive.

Sweet Sixteen, like the other albums before it, went right to gold. Reba explained her continuing success: "My formula, ever since I started sixteen albums ago, was to find the best material possible and make it a great album. I listen to every song a thousand times before I record them, and if I don't get tired of them, I know they're good."

For Reba, life couldn't get much better. She had finally found her Prince Charming—Narvel Blackstock—and they'd decided this love was for keeps.

"No roar of any crowd can compare to your own child saying, 'Mommy, hug me!' That's what's missing from my life."

With just enough time to shoe-horn a wedding into her busy touring schedule, the Queen of Country and her king got married in a sudden hush-hush ceremony that surprised even their closest friends and associates.

Narvel and Reba were married on a boat in the middle of Lake Tahoe on June 3, 1989. The wedding was announced to the world a few days later. "My first marriage was about as public as you can get, so I vowed that when Narvel and I got married, we'd do it as quietly as possible." The lovebirds, who'd been working together ten years (Blackstock worked himself up the ladder from steel guitar player to bandleader to manager), had been talking marriage for a while. "This year," joked Reba, "I've demoted Narvel to husband!"

It hadn't been love at first sight, by any means. "No way," Reba exclaims. "Narvel had three children and had been married a long time. It was just one of those deals where, one day, it was like Wow! When he started working for me back in 1980, I had no idea. Even when we started dating, it was weird, because I never would have picked him as my husband, and he wouldn't have picked me. But the key to it is that we are both very hard workers, and goal-oriented. On vacation, all we talk about is business. We get along really well, we love to work together, and we respect each other. Yep, it's a great marriage."

At the time of the wedding, Reba confided to a friend that her biggest reason for getting married again was to start on a family. She had said repeatedly during her marriage to Charlie Battles that career and family didn't mix, but now Reba changed her tune. A child was definitely on the agenda. "No roar of any crowd can compare to your own child

© Kevin Winter/DMI

A tuxedoed Reba McEntire and husband and manager Narvel Blackstock let fans know that everything is A-OK with them.

© Nick Elgar/London Features

Reba and Narvel out for a night on the town.

saying, 'Mommy, hug me!' That's what's missing from my life," Reba said.

"Reba has been fantastically successful," said a friend, "but true happiness has always eluded her until now."

With her predictably hectic life, Reba got married on a day when she had two shows scheduled. The couple flew twenty family members to Lake Tahoe, Nevada, where Reba was performing. Though the skies were dark and cloudy, the wedding party went cruising on a 41-foot sailboat, *The Woodwind*, for a little over four hours. It was a cool day as well, so guests wrapped themselves in blankets to keep warm while toasting the newlyweds and enjoying a lavish buffet. Reverend Dan Collier, a close friend of Reba's, was on board to perform the twenty-minute marriage ceremony.

Jacqueline McEntire remarked that her daughter was the happiest she'd ever seen her. "Reba looked like a fairy-tale princess—she carried a spray of orchids and put a penny in her shoe for good luck. And Narvel looked so handsome. Every time the two of them decided on a date to get married, something unexpected would come up. The timing now is just perfect. Reba feels ready to balance her career with a family." Somebody on board secretly snapped pictures of the happy couple, and one was sold to *The National Enquirer*, so all of Reba's fans got a chance to get a glimpse of the ultrasecret wedding.

Right after the ceremony, Reba rushed off to do her stage show, then, before the second performance, wedged in a reception—a bite of wedding cake and a toast offered to her and Narvel—with a few friends and bandmates. Reba kept promising everybody that when a baby came along she'd slow down her hectic pace. A friend noted, "Reba said she'd cut down on appearances—especially one-night stands—but she'll sing often enough to keep her fans happy. Reba's even got her nursery all planned. She'll never quit her career, but right now, all she wants to sing are lullabies."

Just weeks after the storybook wedding, the ecstatic singer announced the new partnership was working out famously—she was pregnant with their first child.

Some called the new marriage a show business cliché, a husband masterminding the career of the superstar wife. Some asked if, "having involved ex-husband Charlie Battles in her performing life, was she making the same mistake twice?

Reba said "no." She was absolutely positive that she had made the right choice in every way, personally and professionally: "Narvel entertains me and always has. He makes me work and keeps it all fun and enthusiastic. And he'll be the right kind of daddy. I had to wait for a man who's loving and understanding and giving."

Though the year was filled with more kudos—awards via TNN Viewers' Choice, *Music City News*, and the American Music Awards—the biggest prize was much more personal, a dream come true for the girl who had (almost) everything. When Reba McEntire said she was eager to have a family, she wasn't kidding. Just weeks after the storybook wedding to Narvel Blackstock, the ecstatic singer announced the new partnership was working out famously—she was pregnant with their first child.

Wags figured Reba had probably been expecting on her wedding day. She said it wasn't so. "Just because our marriage took people by surprise, they were whispering. Now that I'm pregnant, they're saying, 'Told you so!' " The baby, due in March, was expressly planned for the period when Reba was in her off-season from touring.

Toward the end of 1989, *Reba Live!* was released—another instant gold record. With a lively cover picture of Reba in performance, dressed head to toe in a gold- and blue-spangled dress, the album contained the message, "Special thanks to all our wonderful fans who made this live album possible. Thanks always for cheering us on. Love, Reba."

Included were songs written by Merle Haggard, Willie Nelson, and Dolly Parton, as well as Reba's best-loved hits: "So, So, So Long"; "One Promise Too Late"; "Let the Music Lift You Up"; "Little Rock"; "New Fool at an Old Game"; "Little Girl"; "Can't Stop Now"; "Sunday Kind of Love"; "I Know How He Feels"; "Whoever's in New England"; "Cathy's Clown"; "You Must Really Love Me"; "Somebody Up There Likes Me"; "San Antonio Rose"; "Mama Tried"; "Night Life"; "Jolene"; "Sweet Dreams"; and "Respect." At the same time, *Reba Home Video* arrived on the market for Christmas, a compilation of McEntire's previous videos, with commentary by the star.

Reba got her good news—"the best thing that ever happened to me"—via an in-home pregnancy test during the last part of her 1989 tour. Narvel, who'd had plenty of baby experience, was just thrilled. "Usually, when you do one of these things [the pregnancy test], it kinda turns a faint pink. Mine just shot right to fuchsia. I was pregnant, all right! It sure is nice when two people are in agreement that they want to have a child and love it forever and ever."

Reba planned to continue performing until Christmas, record her next album in January, then sit back and relax to await the birth of her treasured baby. She gushed to everyone how excited she was about impending motherhood. "I can

Reba throws a Christmas party to celebrate the successes of her stable of Starstruck songwriters.

hardly stand it! This is the news I've been waiting thirty-four years to hear," she said, patting her belly. "My mother always told me I wouldn't know the true joy and happiness of life until I had a child, and she was right. We're redoing the house [the elaborate million-dollar mansion on fifty acres she and Narvel had purchased in Gallatin, Tennessee, on the Cumberland River, not far from Music Row], and I go into the nursery and talk to the baby a lot—he's my buddy. I saw an ultrasound picture, and that's the first time I really knew I was pregnant. Before that, I just felt sick a lot!"

Reba was already planning on an expanded family, saying she wanted four or five kids, though everything would have to fit into the business plan, so as not to jeopardize all the people in her organization. "When this baby is one year and three months old, I wanna get pregnant again. The kids will all have the same birthday month—March—because the first four months of the year are not as good for touring as July through November. I'd love to have four or five more, but I don't know if it's possible, financially or healthwise. I'm thirty-five years old, so we'll see. Narvel's three kids [his seventeen-year-old daughter lives with them; his two sons live in Texas with their mother] are a blast; I love when they come see us!"

Reba was enjoying her pregnancy, and then complications set in. On December 4, the last day of her touring schedule for the year, she visited her doctor and learned that her cervix was thinning. Told she'd have to spend some time "flat on her back" to guard against a dangerously premature birth, Reba became alarmed. After a holiday visit to Oklahoma to see her family, McEntire returned to Nashville and checked into the hospital on January 15. The plans to record her new album had to be postponed, with a new date set for sometime in April after the baby was born.

Reba was prepared to make any sacrifice necessary to protect the health of her child. "I was having contractions, so they put me on asthma medicine to stop them. I was in bed for a long time. It was hard laying in bed by myself for thirteen or fourteen hours a day, with nothing to do but listen to music, read, and watch TV, but I knew it was best for the baby. I was real worried, but it all worked out fine."

RUMOR HAS IT 17

The enforced peace, quiet, and solitude had a profound effect on Reba's next album, *Rumor Has It.* With so much time on her hands, she had months and months to listen to hundreds of songs. She also needed time to shop around and find herself a new producer—her collaboration with Jimmy Bowen had come to a forced end when he switched over from Reba's label, MCA, to Capitol Nashville. After interviewing many different producers, Reba picked Tony Brown. "I met with Tony last. What I wanted and what he wanted was the same. We've always gotten along really well—he's easy to work with and has energy. Tony brings a lot of life to the music, and he coached me. I thoroughly enjoyed working with him and look forward to the next album."

With the radio on all the time ("If I played it too loud, Shelby would squirm around and kick me!"), Reba listened to a lot of contemporary music—Phil Collins, Steve Winwood, Don Henley, Tina Turner. "I'd compare their records, their bass sounds [a lot of them use a bass synthesizer], and I wanted to see how that stuff would enhance my music and make it richer. Not louder, just richer."

She used the experience to study trends in pop radio music, trying to figure out what kind of sound was the most commercial, and especially what people were buying and who was getting the most play. "I listened to Michael Bolton a lot. His sound is so alive and intense. I got to comparing his vocals to mine. Not his music or songs, just the vocals. I started to feel I wasn't putting enough into it. I wanted a more energized, intense sound."

Before she was forced into bed, Reba had been going to a lot of pop concerts—George Michael was her favorite. All this exposure to contemporary music definitely had its effect. "Some of my songs can be sweet and wimpy, but with *Rumor Has It,* I think I put more raw energy into it. There's been a progression. After *Reba,* I kind of took a step back toward traditional music with *Sweet Sixteen.* The *Live* album showed what we had done over the last ten years. Then, this one [*Rumor Has It*] is a step back toward straight ahead NOW. I wouldn't call it traditional or contemporary, I'd call it hip."

During the course of her pregnancy, Reba got pitched literally hundreds of baby songs, none of which made it onto the record. She had no interest in a "baby album"—having a child was a very private thing to her. The album was business, and even though it was difficult, given her physical and emotional state, she kept her focus on organizing the new record.

Shelby Steven McEntire Blackstock, weighing in at 6 pounds 10 ounces, was welcomed into the

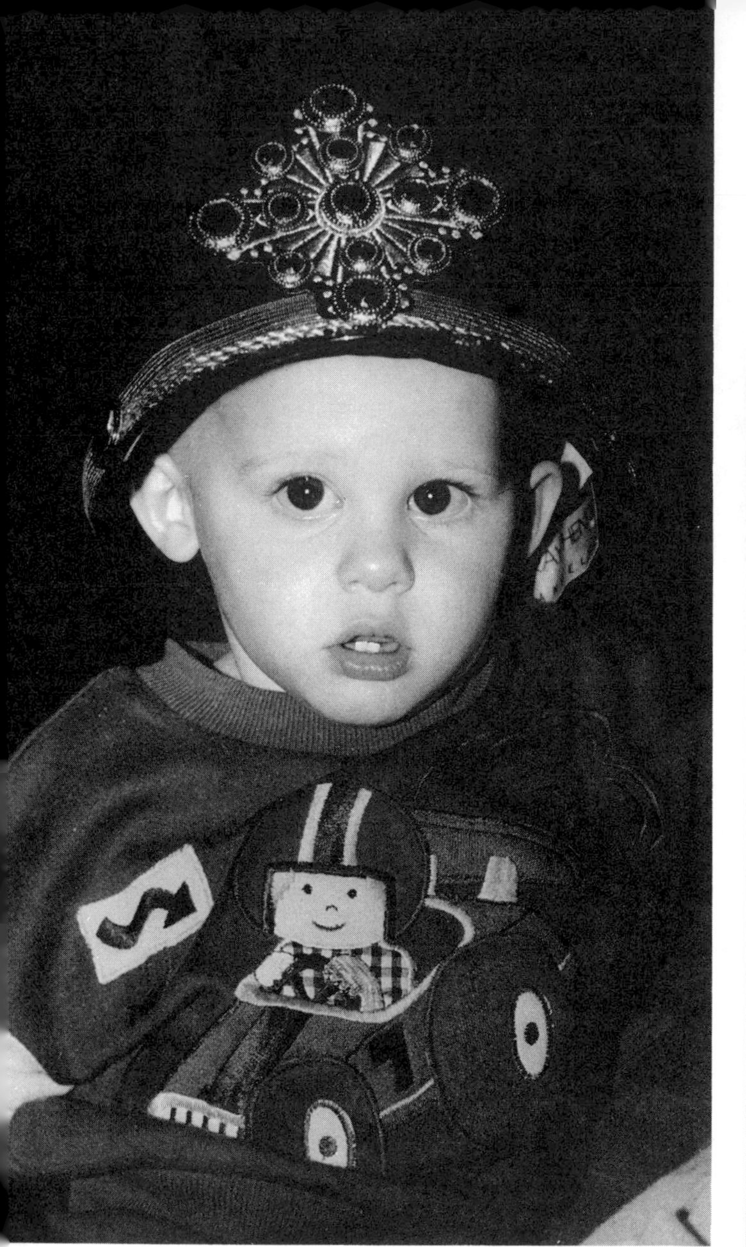

© Ron Wolfson/London Features

Country's royal baby—
Shelby.

© Ron Wolfson/London Features

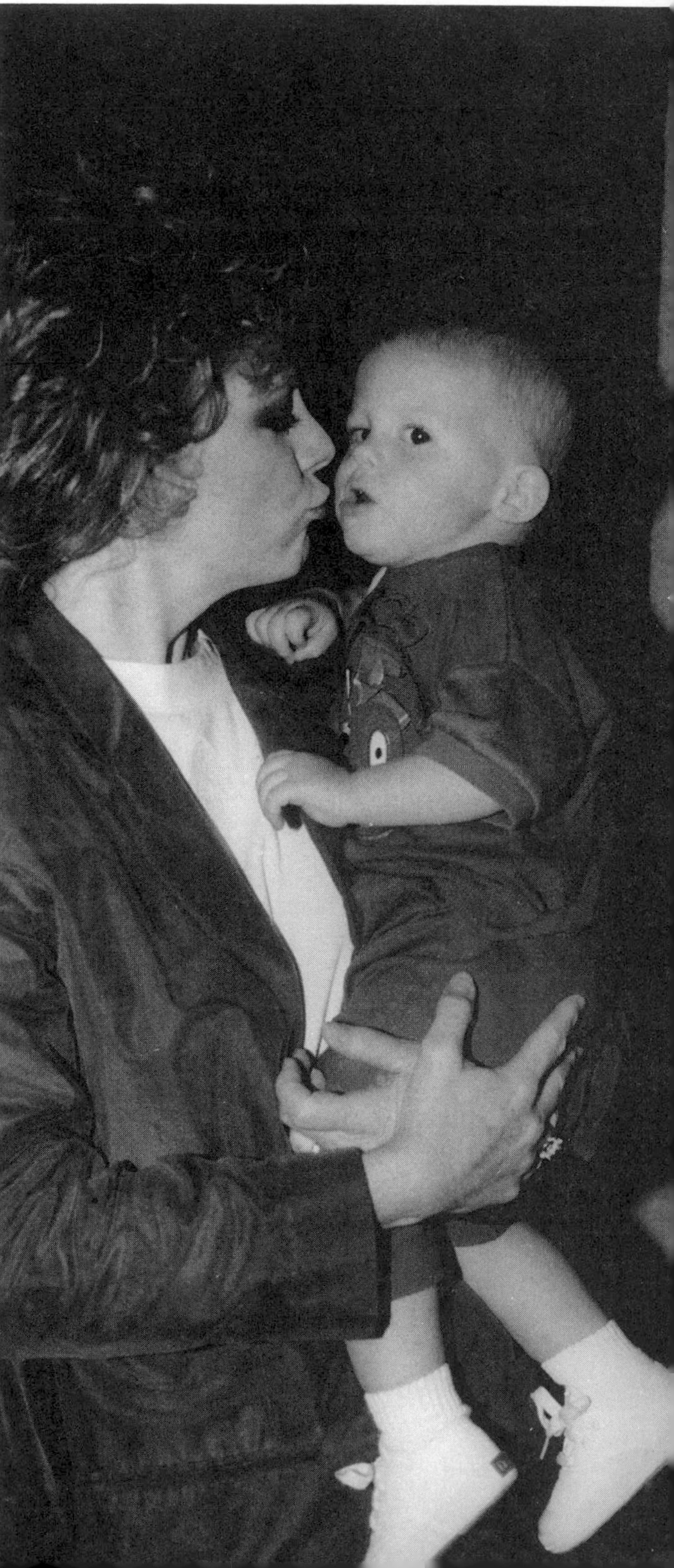

A kiss for her favorite fan!

world on February 23, 1990, at West Side Hospital in Nashville. His arrival was two weeks early. Being a mom was everything Reba had hoped for, and she fell madly and instantly in love with her son.

McEntire's "warm, supple voice" survived childbirth with no appreciable damage, unlike other Nashville singing mothers, who'd been experiencing their own baby boom. Pregnant vocalists had been talking about temporary huskiness and lowered tone that hormonal changes sometimes bring, but Reba was surprised by the idea. She even felt she might have gained a note or two!

Like an advertisement for the woman who has it all, Reba was back in shape and on the road by May. The highly disciplined superstar organized her life down to the last detail, so that she could juggle career and family to perfection (without much time to adjust to being a mom). She was soon in the studio recording *Rumor Has It.* While motherhood was the best and most fulfilling experience of her life, Reba, a self-described workaholic, couldn't help but be concerned about her career. Her record sales had declined (though not substantially) during her brief absence from the music scene. Aware of how fickle the public can be, and afraid that the audience might forget about her, a worried McEntire hit the road in a big way, returning to her usual grueling schedule. She had no intention of letting a decade of intensely hard work fall by the wayside. "You always have to plan in this business, especially since I have so many people on the payroll who are depending on me."

One of McEntire's first "post-Shelby" gigs was with Garth Brooks, undeniably the hottest phenomenon in both country and pop music today. (His debut album boosted him from obscurity to the top of every chart, and he's gone multi-platinum since.) Reba and her band were working Tuesdays through Sundays, sometimes doing two shows a day. "I'm playing catch-up for the time I was off having Shelby. This is the longest I've ever been off the road—five months. You've got to stay out there, or [the fans] will go to Patty Loveless, Kathy Mattea, Lorrie Morgan. It's like 'out of sight, out of mind,' and I don't blame 'em. Touring sells records, so I'm going out there."

Even with this almost maniacal return to work, Reba's dedication to family life was unshakeable. "Some of the things I used to think were important—now they can wait." Shelby never got the chance to miss his mother, who joined the "jet set" after his birth. Reba and Narvel, in order to streamline their schedule and be able to commute back and forth between Nashville and her live shows, bought a seven-seat Sabre jet, even though friend Barbara Mandrell ("She's like my bossy big sister!") warned Reba that she would miss touring on the bus. "Barbara and her husband came over for dinner one night and landed their helicopter right on my front lawn. I told her I did like flying—a lot—and she didn't believe me."

Jetting around allows Reba and Narvel to get home to see the baby every night, and get up early for their "morning routine" with Shelby, who is then turned over to the care of his nanny, Cindy. Reba is then free to go off to her daily round of meetings at Starstruck, although she acknowledges she's always eager to get back home.

"Now we can leave for a show at around six in the evening," Reba explained. "Then we go in and meet all the folks we need to, do the show, and visit with the local fan club members." (There are some 20,000 of them nationally.)

© Walter McBride/Retna Ltd.

A very '90s mom—juggling a career and a family.

"Afterwards, we fly back home. The latest we ever got back into Nashville was four A.M.—and that was from Portland, Oregon. From the East Coast, with the hour-earlier time difference, you're home by midnight."

It's exhausting, to be sure, but Reba continues to thrive on the excitement of her whirlwind career and the obvious focal point of it all, her son. She also loves to be home in the comfort of her own bed, with her own pillow and blanket.

Sometimes Shelby travels right along with his parents. "We just troop along. In the summers, when he's older, he'll travel with us all the time, just like I did with my daddy. We had a blast!" During a two-week swing on the West Coast, Reba rented a house in Carmel, on the California coast, making that her home base. It was all very "Lifestyles of the Rich and Famous," which seemed appropriate for Reba, who, with her movie debut in 1990, has her eyes trained on Hollywood as the next territory to conquer.

With the release of *Rumor Has It* (the singer termed it "the best album I've ever done"), Reba scored her sixth consecutive gold album, celebrated by a huge billboard in the middle of prestigious Sunset Boulevard in Los Angeles. It was an album all about change—change in her sound, her look, and the state of her life.

The front cover of the album features a very sophisticated, chic, "dolled-up" Reba, sporting perfect nails and wearing a sleek tangerine dress and diamond bracelet, with a '50s-style hat/scarf combination reminiscent of the early Debbie Reynolds. ("I once flew out to L.A. sitting in a seat right in front of Debbie, but I was way too shy to talk to her," confessed Reba on a recent talk show.) A small photo on the back of the album shows a casual yet voluptuous and beaming Reba. Both poses are obvious statements of just how far she has come from her days as a tentative Okie cowgirl in blue jeans and sporting a big rodeo buckle.

As has become her tradition, Reba offers a personal message on *Rumor Has It:* "Special thanks to all the writers, musicians and singers whose talents really shine on these songs," it begins. She then acknowledges a number of people in her Starstruck organization, and concludes with thanks: "To my band and road crew—you're the best! To the fans, DJ's and folks who sell our music—thanks so much, we couldn't do it without you! To my manager, husband, friend and partner—Narvel, thanks for the great ideas, the long hours of discussions and for taking care of me all these years. Thank God for Shelby, who put everything in a different perspective."

Although she's singing a lot of pop tunes now, Reba will never leave country. "Listen to the way I talk!"

With the release of *Rumor Has It*, Reba scored her sixth consecutive gold album, celebrated by a huge billboard in the middle of prestigious Sunset Boulevard. It was an album all about change . . .

While the disc doesn't contain outright rock or soul, it's far from traditional country—very pop, with synthesizers and heavy-duty backing vocals. There's no sign of a steel guitar or fiddle anywhere.

Reba found this recording experience intense. "I'd been off the road, I was fresh." In some ways, her style of performance harkens back to the early days of her career, when she was forced into a more contemporary sound that was, in her judgment, wrong for her then. This record has her forging toward mainstream contemporary music.

The style of this record led to endless discussions among critics and fans alike. Some felt that Reba's pop material was nowhere near as good as her traditional country, while others worried that she had become preoccupied with the business, rather than focused on the music itself, and would "define herself as nothing more than the sum total of her audiences' expectations." *The Nashville Banner* called her stage performance in support of the new album "merely a wisp of country in Reba's fancy new show."

But Reba wasn't worried. She matured and now possessed an inner peace and self-assuredness that she'd never had before. There were no apologies forthcoming about the pop style this time. "This record is a progression," she said. It's a change and changes are necessary. I do believe that if you shock them and go past where they want you to go, they'll get used to you in the new light. My audience has accepted me."

Record sales proved she was right. "I want to do what sells. I want to do what the majority of the public likes to hear, and this is it. Some people say they want me to go back to singing traditional, but when I do, I can't get the big numbers on those records."

© Bruno Gaget/Retna Ltd.

Reba was excited by producer Tony Brown's fresh approach on *Rumor Has It.* "I'm not a musician, I'm a singer. Jimmy Bowen always wanted me to work on arrangements and I've done that for eight albums. This time, I just wanted to have fun and sing like it was a stage show," making the finished product twice as lively as usual.

The record's hit single, the fastest-moving of Reba's entire career, "You Lie," was immediately dubbed a Nashville classic—a "heart-touching ballad that's ninety percent pop and ten percent country." Reba wrings the emotion out of her voice on this one about a shattered marriage.

The absolute gem of the album, however, is "Fancy," a song that ruled the charts when Bobby Gentry first wrote and recorded it in 1969. The song, about a girl who was forced into prostitution by her mother, was made for Reba's gutsy style. "I always loved that song, and always wanted to do it," said Reba, whose career has thrived on songs with a strong and uplifting message. "I think so many people can relate to 'Fancy' because, though it has a sad beginning, it points out that we can always rise above our situations if we put our heart and mind into doing so." Reba's video version of the song still continues to get heavy rotation on cable music channel VH-1.

McEntire's only writing contribution to the album is "Climb That Mountain High," a pop-flavored tune about making it in a hard world that she cowrote with Don Schlitz. More in her usual vein is the title track, "Rumor Has It," one of the standouts on the album. It's a ballad drenched in heartbreak, all about a woman who hears people gossiping that her man is in love with another woman.

"Waitin' for the Deal to Go Down" is a western-tinged rock number about a girl who's waiting for her man to put that ring on her finger. He keeps saying it's going to happen, but she's beginning to suspect that he's not telling the truth, that she's in for some heartbreak.

In "Now You Tell Me," the man has waited too long to tell his woman that he's in love with her. She's involved with someone new, after going crazy waiting for him. Now it's too late.

"Fallin' Out of Love" is a sad song about a breakup that's all for the best. It's hard on both the

Hoping to conquer Hollywood, country and pop star Reba goes for a more sophisticated image.

people in the relationship, but now they can get on with their lives. Obviously, Reba's newly found personal happiness didn't prevent her from giving expression to older sad memories.

"This Picture," featuring a strong rock and roll backbeat, is the tale of a feisty woman ready to forget the man who's left her. She may be ready—

she's ripped up his picture—but his memory still haunts her.

"You Remember Me" is a delicate ballad written by 1960s folk-rocker Jesse Winchester, all about how two old lovers meet and remember the good times and the bad. The album closes with a hard-rocking number, "That's All She Wrote," this one a story of a cheating man who comes home with his tail between his legs because his new woman has dumped him. The woman he left originally takes him back—she still loves him.

Having acted in videos and on TV, Reba was a welcome guest on many of the talk shows; she displayed a lovable and entertaining combination of "sweetness and salty humor." She headed for Hollywood, determined to test herself as an actress. She had been trying for some years, but had never had the clout to get producers and directors to cast her. "They always wanted Meg Ryan whenever I tried to get a part," she complained. But she was not about to give up her acting ambitions.

It took two readings, but Miss McEntire made her big screen debut in a campy science-fiction horror/comedy called *Tremors,* all about giant subterranean creatures who invade a small town. Costarring with Michael Gross (of TV's "Family Ties"), Kevin Bacon, and Fred Ward, Reba portrayed Heather, the strong wife of an eccentric survivalist (Gross); she helps her husband blow away a couple of the man-eating monsters with an arsenal of weapons—"Don't forget your Swiss cheese and your bullets, dear!"

Reba found acting pretty easy. "They didn't have much for me in my part, then we started to ad-lib,

Reba is always a welcome guest on the talk show circuit because of her friendly sense of humor.

Reba McEntire cohosts "Good Morning America" with regular anchor Charles Gibson in Oklahoma City—to celebrate the history of the state.

The fans fill the stands to get a good look at their favorite female country singer.

Reba welcomes Roger Miller to the outdoor stage set of "Good Morning America."

© Capital Cities/ABC, Inc. (Lisa Rudy)

Set against the Oklahoma City skyline, Roger Miller strums a good ole country tune.

© Capital Cities/ABC, Inc. (Lisa Rudy)

and it got bigger—I'm such a stage ham. I didn't want to play Reba McEntire or a country singer. I even got to shoot guns!"

Though she was "ready to go back to music when the movie was finished, I'd do it again," said Reba. "As a pretty disciplined person who is usually in control of my own organization, movie-making was a frustrating experience—not the acting but the waiting around"—a common complaint of many novice actors.

Tremors didn't rock the movie world, but McEntire got good reviews and the film became a top ten video rental. Reba was slotted to write and record part of the movie's soundtrack, but she and the producers couldn't agree on the financial arrangements, so she kept the tunes for her album instead.

Movie and TV roles seem to be Reba's next career move, but not a TV series—"I don't want to do a show like Dolly Parton or Barbara Mandrell did. I think I'd get bored too quick. What I love is live TV."

Quality-control is all-important, as McEntire quickly learned. "If some big studio operation like Disney or Universal came to me with a contract to do movies, and up-front money, I wouldn't just sign on the dotted line—I'd ask to see the scripts first." Reba has signed up with the prestigious Triad Agency for movie and television representation, and spends a great deal of time in Los Angeles, making the rounds to see producers and directors. She's also landed legendary literary agent Swifty Lazar, and is discussing possible writing projects.

After filling in for vacationing Joan Lunden on ABC's "Good Morning, America" (on which she's been a frequent guest) in a show that focused on the history of Oklahoma, and a performance at the

© Susan Biddle/The White House

Even though the country is about to go to war in the Middle East, President Bush has time to win over a new constituent, Shelby Blackstock, as his mother and father look on with pride.

© Susan Biddle/The White House

In Washington, D.C., for a performance, McEntire—along with husband, Narvel, and son, Shelby—accepts an invitation to visit the White House from rabid country fan George Bush.

Goodwill Games in Seattle, Reba headed to Washington, D.C., to appear with Larry King on his radio and TV talk shows.

Alerted to the fact that Reba was in town, the President and Mrs. Bush extended an invitation to "their favorite country singer" to visit the White House, even though George Bush was working on his nationally televised speech condemning Iraq's invasion of Kuwait. Accompanied by Narvel and Shelby, the singer and her family were given a twenty-minute tour of the First Family's private quarters in the White House by Mrs. Bush, who also introduced them to the First Dog, Millie, and Millie's son Ranger. "I really enjoyed meeting them, it was an honor," Reba said later. "Considering all the President had on his mind, it was very gracious of them to take time to make us feel right at home."

Taking home her fourth consecutive American Music Award for "Favorite Female Country Vocalist," Reba missed out on a fifth honor at the Academy of Country Music show in Los Angeles. Instead she proudly showed off her biggest prize, Shelby Blackstock, to the TV audience.

Being a superwoman all the time is impossible, even for the usually invincible Reba McEntire. On February 16, 1991, she was forced to check herself into the H.C.A. Donelson Hospital in suburban Nashville. It was just four days before a scheduled appearance in New York City at the Grammys. Extremely run-down, Reba was suffering from bronchitis, a severe throat infection, and nodules and blisters on her vocal cords (this last problem had become chronic for Reba over the years). Her doctor, Richard Quisling, treated her for an infection causing inflammation and swelling of the nasal passages, larynx, and trachea.

Unwilling to disappoint her fans, who expected McEntire to present an award at the Grammys with Randy Travis, a hard-driving Reba dragged herself out of the hospital against "everybody's advice," and flew to New York. She and Narvel checked into their Plaza Hotel suite on Fifth Avenue facing Central Park. Reba went to bed, figuring that a good night's sleep would make her feel better. The next morning, her condition had severely worsened. Blackstock begged Reba to skip the show, where she was nominated for "Female Vocalist of the Year" (Kathy Mattea turned out to be the winner in that category). A local doctor was called for a pre-

In the ten years of the '80s, Reba won a lifetime of awards, more than any other country star in history.

© Steve Granitz/Retna Ltd.

scription to ease the swelling, and a painkiller was administered.

Getting ready for an 11 A.M. rehearsal, Reba collapsed unconscious in her hotel room, after complaining of dizziness. Narvel came out of the bathroom to find her passed-out on the floor. She revived about a half-minute later. The doctor returned, and wanted to send Reba immediately to the hospital. She was insistent about going to the Grammys, but her husband refused to hear of it. "I know the Grammys mean a lot to you, but you mean more to me and our baby. I love you and I'm taking you home to get well."

The couple returned immediately to Nashville, where Reba spent only two days in bed before leaving to keep a tour date in Lake Charles, Louisiana. Close friends of the couple were worried that Reba was systematically ruining her voice and her health from pushing too hard. "Reba doesn't want to lose her grip on the top rung of the country music ladder," confided a friend. "Her hectic schedule is even more strenuous because of little Shelby. It's a demonstration of love that she flies back to Nashville every night, but it just might be too much."

In spite of her episode with bronchitis and everybody's concern over her health, there seemed little that could stop the superstar at this point. And then something did—a terrible twist of fate, a tragedy so horrible it completely shattered Reba's storybook life and snuffed out the lives of eight people she loved dearly.

18 TRAGEDY STRIKES

Reba McEntire, enjoying a golden career, a picture-perfect family life, and a healthy dose of good luck, remained tireless in her desire to expand her audience. That's why she accepted an invitation from IBM to perform a concert for their "top performers" in San Diego on Friday, March 15, 1991. Because she was in the middle of a tour through the Midwest, McEntire, as was her usual practice, arranged to fly in and out of San Diego the same day in order to be back in Fort Wayne, Indiana, in time for a Saturday night concert there. Her band, who usually traveled by bus, was forced to take to the air as well, in order to arrive on time for the next gig.

The seventy-five-minute IBM concert at the Sheraton Harbor Island Hotel was a hit, with Reba once again performing Patsy Cline's "Sweet Dreams" as an encore. Seven members of the band and Reba's tour manager, Jim Hammon, flew out of San Diego's Brown Field early Saturday morning in a twin-engine Hawker Siddeley private jet owned

Celebrating Christmas with former road manager Jim Hammon, who later perished in the tragic plane crash that killed eight members of Reba's band.

by Duncan Aircraft of Venice, Florida. A refueling stop was scheduled for Amarillo, Texas, with Fort Wayne as the ultimate destination.

At 1:40 A.M. on March 16, the plane's wing clipped an outcropping of rock near the 3,572-foot peak of the Otay Mountains—to the east of San Diego's Brown Field. The jet, which investigators believe was traveling at 200 miles per hour, cartwheeled and smashed into the side of the mountain, exploding upon impact. There were no survivors. Almost immediately after takeoff, personnel at the Navy's North Island Naval Air Station, reported seeing a fireball just twenty-five miles southeast of downtown San Diego. Mercifully, the passengers on board probably had no idea what was happening and were killed instantly.

Reba was supposed to have been on the ill-fated plane that night, but because of her recent health problems (she was still suffering from bronchitis), her husband, Narvel, had urged her to stay in San Diego and get a good night's rest. The couple were fast asleep and unaware of the tragedy when local police arrived at the crash site, just about a mile from the Mexican border. Fuel was still burning, and debris was scattered for hundreds of yards over the rough countryside. "It was a grisly scene," said Sergeant Michael O'Connor of the San Diego sheriff's office. "Clothing and bits and pieces of broken musical instruments were everywhere." Many of the volunteers who searched for remains of the bodies found the experience so upsetting that it was necessary to bring in a psychologist to comfort them.

The Federal Aviation Agency official at the site, Richard Childress, could not immediately figure out why the plane had gone down. "It just disappeared," he said. "Though there was good visibility, it's possible that the pilot just didn't see the mountain." The National Transportation Safety Board began an immediate investigation into the tragedy, but no matter what their conclusion, it was too late for the ten victims.

The dead included the pilot, Captain Don Holms, and First Officer Chris Hollinger, along with Jim Hammon, forty, of Nashville, a one-time t-shirt salesman who'd worked his way up in the McEntire organization to become tour manager; Kirk Capella, twenty-eight, of Florisant, Missouri, a former musical director for Barbara Mandrell and Reba's current bandleader and keyboards player; Paula Kaye Evans, thirty-three, of Nashville, one of Reba's backup singers, who had just recently joined the band; Chris Austin, twenty-seven, of Boone, North Carolina, another backup singer and one of the McEntire stable of songwriters, who'd previously played for Ricky Skaggs; Tony Saputo, thirty-four, of St. Louis, Missouri, the band's drummer; Terry Jackson, twenty-eight, of Los Angeles, California, a bass-player who had at one time toured with pop singer Thomas Dolby; Joey Cigainero, twenty-seven, of Jacksonville, Texas, a keyboardist; and Michael Thomas, thirty-four, of Loganville, Indiana, a guitarist who had once been a member of the T. Graham Brown band. That left only two surviving band members, Joe McGlohon and Pete Finney. They had taken off from the same airfield in a second jet, only minutes behind the doomed plane.

Reba and Narvel were awakened around 2:30 that morning by their pilot, who asked Narvel to come to his room. As he dressed quickly, Narvel told Reba, "I think there's been an accident," but urged her to go back to sleep. Of course, she couldn't and waited for her husband to return. He did, with the horrible, mind-numbing news that the plane had gone down.

© Steve Lowry/Nashville Banner

A somber Reba and Narvel leave the church where funeral services were held for McEntire's eight bandmates killed in the plane crash of March 16, 1991.

"It was a nightmare from then on. We were hoping and praying that there might be some survivors," said Reba. "Eventually, we radioed the second plane carrying the crew and Joe and Pete. They got off their plane for a refueling stop in Memphis and were told about the tragedy." After initially refusing to get back on their plane, the grief-stricken survivors returned to Nashville.

Reba, who later described the ordeal in an interview on "Entertainment Tonight," said her mind was paralyzed. She desperately wanted to believe that a call would come saying it had all been a bad dream. For hours she held onto that shred of hope, until it was confirmed that the Hawker Siddeley had gone down, and that there were no survivors. All that was left were the plane's Rolls Royce engines.

After a thorough investigation by the FAA into the plane crash that took the lives of McEntire's band, it was announced that a misunderstanding between the pilot and the air traffic controller may have led to the accident. It was impossible to document the cause of the crash because there was no "black box" flight recorder on board. Taped conversations released by the FAA showed that pilot Don Holms contacted a flight service specialist based at city-owned Montgomery Field, twenty-five miles away, for information regarding departure procedures three times before his takeoff from Brown Field. Holms was questioning the proper altitude to maintain after takeoff. Transcripts revealed that the flight specialist said yes when the pilot asked if he should stay below 3,000 feet. There seems to have been some confusion in the flight specialist's mind as to whether the pilot meant feet above ground level or sea level, and the lack of communication proved to be fatal.

It's a sad occasion, but Reba smiles as the audience reaches out to comfort her at the memorial concert held to aid the families of the lost bandmates.

It was a hard thing to do, but Reba wanted to pay tribute to her lost loved ones. She makes a surprise performance at the memorial concert in Nashville, which brought out the cream of country stardom.

"It was by far my darkest hour. The most awful thing that ever happened in my life," Reba says. "When you have eight people that you absolutely love, and their lives are just wiped out—it's devastating." Two days after the disaster, Reba gave a phone interview (from her home) to a *People* magazine reporter who was a close friend. "The story needed to be told, and I wanted to make sure it would be done right, with a protective attitude toward the families."

As if the weather were responding to the tragic event, it rained all that day. Narvel called all of the families to tell them their loved ones would not be coming home. Reba recalled sadly, "It was so hard for him to do that. How do you tell a daddy that his boy is dead? How do you tell a wife her husband may not be coming home, or a husband that his wife is gone?"

Reba and Narvel returned to Nashville Friday night, stopping off at home first to check on Shelby. Then they headed straight over to Jim Hammon's wife, Debbie, and their two sons, to offer condolences and a shoulder to cry on. Reba told Debbie she couldn't go back on the road without her bandmates, her family. Debbie asked the singer if she was thinking about quitting for good. "I said, 'Well, no, but I don't know when I can go back.' "

A grief-stricken but brave Debbie replied, "Jim Hammon worked all this time to help you get where you are today. He'd kick your butt if you thought about quitting."

After a quiet embrace and a lot of tears, Reba thanked Debbie for the words of encouragement, given in the midst of Debbie's own devastating loss. Reba and Narvel first canceled their tour arrangements, then spent all weekend visiting with the band members' families, offering support and comfort, even though they themselves were in a daze, hurting badly.

Sometimes people who survive a tragedy feel guilty. Worried that Reba might experience this emotion, Waylon Jennings, who was on tour with Buddy Holly when that legendary singer died in a plane crash in the early 1960s, called to offer Reba some guidance and helpful words. "Don't let guilt set in, don't even let it touch you. There's nothing you could have done," he counseled.

It was more than a little eerie that Reba would be spared the fate of her singing idol, while her band perished in so similar an incident.

The Nashville music community, devastated by country's biggest loss since the death of Patsy Cline, Cowboy Copas, and Hawkshaw Hawkins in a fiery mountainside plane crash in 1963, rallied around its own with immediate care, concern, and compassion. It was more than a little eerie that Reba would be spared the fate of her singing idol, while her band perished in so similar an incident. Making an appearance on "The Oprah Winfrey Show" six or seven months after the tragedy, Reba spoke of the outpouring of support from the Nashville music community: "Sometimes we can be a competitive bunch, but when somebody's in trouble, everybody helps out."

Country stations all over the United States broadcast dedications to the dead musicians; letters from people worried about Reba poured in from everywhere. Merle Haggard, Lorrie Morgan, Lee Greenwood, Janie Fricke, Kathy Mattea, Charlie Daniels, and Sawyer Brown donated their services to cover concerts McEntire and her band had scheduled to perform in Illinois. More than $100,000 was raised through those appearances and divided among the families who had lost their loved ones. More big-name talent organized a benefit show for April 22 at Nashville's Municipal Auditorium to raise even more cash for the survivors. Featured were Kenny Rogers, the Oak Ridge Boys, T. Graham Brown, Gary Morris, Exile, Patty Loveless, and Eddie Rabbitt. Reba organized several funds to provide aid for the families, as did Capitol Records and the American Federation of Musicians, based in Nashville.

While these fund-raising events were taking place, there was a more important agenda to be dealt with. The victims had to be laid to rest. Southwest Airlines provided free transportation for bereaved family members to the memorial service in Nashville. On March 20 at Christ Church in Brentwood, Tennessee, Reba and Narvel, along with other Music City luminaries like Barbara Mandrell, Kathy Mattea, Ricky Skaggs, Naomi and Wynonna Judd, Larry Strickland, Vince Gill, Larry Gatlin, Steve Wariner, June Carter Cash, Garth Brooks, Skeeter Davis, Charlie Dick (husband of the late Patsy Cline), and Tennessee Governor Ned Ray McWherter gathered together for the somber memorial service. The Reverend Dan Scott conducted the service, reading the Ninety-first Psalm, one of Reba's favorites, to provide some comfort to the mourners.

Johnny Cash, who had been asked specifically by Reba to speak at the service, talked about burying his own mother only a week before. Worried that performing the next day might have seemed disrespectful, he had discussed the matter with friend Willie Nelson (recently suffering his own tragedy—his son hanged himself right after Christmas of 1991), who replied, "It's our way of life, and our way of dealing with pain." Then Cash performed an acoustic version of the Cindy Walker song "Jim I Wore a Tie Today," substituting each of the dead band members' names, ending with the sad but inspirational line, "When you get to the streets of gold, stake a claim for me." Johnny ended his part of the service with a recitation of Hank Williams' "Negro Funeral."

A strange thing happened that allowed Reba to have a special remembrance of her lost loved ones. At the San Diego concert, a member of the audience had taped the band's last show together, even though such taping is prohibited. The tape had been turned over to Narvel, and Reba now has an important memento of that last, fateful show.

"Evidently, I was not meant to go on that plane. . . . God must have things for me to do."

"Evidently, I was not meant to go on that plane," Reba has said. "God must have things for me to do. Maybe it's because of our baby. Maybe that's why Joe McGlohon wasn't on that plane either—his wife just had a baby. And Pete Finney. He switched at the last minute with Michael Thomas. Michael is gone, but Pete is here with us today. There are reasons." Saying she might never be able to sing the prophetic "Sweet Dreams" again, Reba told Vince Gill that she couldn't bear to turn around and see that her friends were gone. Feeling almost unable to cope, Reba pushed herself to appear at the Academy Awards ceremony, making her appearance a tribute to her lost loved ones.

On the advice of friends, Reba went right back to work. Later she said she did so for her sanity—if she'd had too much time to sit around and think about her lost friends, "it would have eaten me up inside."

Good friend Dolly Parton called to offer Reba her band, her crew, anything she needed. In fact, it was Dolly's bandleader and manager, Gary Smith, who put together a new group of musicians to play with Reba upon her return to work. Reba announced she would resume performing on April 7 at the Richfield Coliseum in Ohio.

Steve Rosenblatt, manager of the venue, was surprised that McEntire was keeping to her schedule. "It's an awfully short time for her to get a band together, both physically and emotionally," he said. But Reba, always the trouper, announced that the show, with McEntire and Clint Black headlining, supported by Vince Gill, would go on. At every stop on her itinerary, the audiences welcomed Reba with an outpouring of love, applauding her decision to sing. For Reba, it was a slow road back—"Everything's a reminder"—but her strength of character and devotion to work and family kept her going. And going. And going.

Reba McEntire's nineteenth album, *For My Broken Heart*, was recorded after the plane crash and reflected the singer's sadness over the death of the members of her band. Almost every cut on the album is a tearjerker. "When you're in a state of grief like I am, you pick sad songs," Reba said. "I don't think I'll ever stop grieving." The album contained a little note to Reba's fans: "It seems your current emotional state determines what music you'd like to hear. That's what happened on the song selection for this album. If for any reason you can relate to the emotion packed inside, I hope it's a form of healing for all our broken hearts."

Reba's intense grief is reflected on the cover photo of *For My Broken Heart.* Two other pictures that accompany the song lyrics show her looking happier, but wistful just the same. The album is a perfect marriage of pop and country—Reba does justice to both styles, and her voice, dripping with pain on every cut, never sounded better. Many of the songs deal with lost love and survival, feelings obviously close to Reba's heart at the time. But the album also takes on many issues that affect our daily lives, and, more than ever, focuses on concerns Reba shares with other women, "her best friends."

The title track, written by two songwriters from the Starstruck stable, is a sad but stunningly beautiful song about the breakup of a love that was supposed to last forever. The woman left behind can barely stumble through her miserable existence, but after some time passes, she realizes that life goes on. To accompany this song, Reba shot a very moving video featuring an older housewife, a businesswoman, and a teenage girl, all of them going through troubling times. The video ends with Reba walking into the sunlight, smiling a tentative but hopeful smile, assuring us that everything will be all right.

A mixture of pop and western swing, "Is There Life Out There?" has a woman who jumped into a marriage at twenty wondering if she's missed out on too much. She doesn't want to leave her husband and family, but she's just dying to do something wild and crazy.

"Bobby," a song cowritten by Reba McEntire, is a story song, very much in the country tradition, about a husband who kills his wife. The man's little son hopes his father burns in hell, but when the boy grows up and falls in love, he understands. His mother had suffered a horrible accident that left

© Alan L. Mayor

A heartfelt version of "For My Broken Heart," sung at the 1991 Country Music Awards at the Grand Ole Opry.

© Steve Granitz/Retna Ltd.

Her performance at the Country Music Awards entrances the live audience and television viewers all over the world.

her an invalid and in terrible pain, and his father killed her because he loved her so much that he didn't want to see her suffer.

A good, old-fashioned country ballad, "He's in Dallas" has a wife taking the baby and leaving her husband. He had promised he'd be a good husband, but he broke his promises and his wife's heart. Now she's going home, afraid to break the news to her mama, who's getting older and worries too much. "All Dressed Up (with Nowhere to Go)" has an old woman in a retirement home feeling her life is already over. Her family never visits, but she gets all dressed up anyway, and just sits alone, with no place to go.

The album's string of sad songs continues with Reba's remake of the 1970s pop hit "The Night the Lights Went Out in Georgia." The singer tells a long story about finding her lover with her brother's cheating wife. Her brother takes the rap for her and is hanged, even though she has committed the two murders of her lover and her brother's tramp wife.

"Buying Her Roses" could almost be a Beatles tune, all about a woman so busy with her job and the kids that she has taken her husband for granted. So her husband has found a lover, somebody who needs him. The wife doesn't know whether to fight for him or let him go. Sadly, neither choice sounds as if it will have a happy ending. "The Greatest Man I Never Knew" is a ballad about a woman's almost nonexistent relationship with her dead husband. She never realized how much he loved her until it was too late.

"I Wouldn't Go That Far" is about an old relationship and a love that might have been. It tells of two young people who were in love, but the girl wasn't ready to make a commitment. She let the relationship slip away. When the two of them run into each other years later, he's married and she's become famous, and while they wonder what might have been, they're both happy for each other.

The final song on the album, "If I'd Only Known," is a soaring, painful song about losing somebody you love before you're ready. It deals with death that comes without warning, and is obviously dedicated to Reba's lost band. Her voice is chilling and beautiful, melding soulfully with an affecting string arrangement.

On October 2, 1991, Reba Nell McEntire played host to the twenty-fifth anniversary broadcast of the Country Music Awards, televised live on CBS from the Grand Ole Opry. Resplendent in a turquoise-spangled dress and with the requisite giant Nashville hairdo, a proud and beaming Reba, nominated for three awards, was privileged to welcome the event's special guests. In the audience were President and Barbara Bush, the first time a President of the United States had ever attended the awards ceremony. In its welcome to the Bushes, the crowd offered up a standing ovation. In her Oklahoma accent, so thick you could cut it with a knife, Reba introduced the evening's presenters and performers, who included Roy Rogers and Dolly Parton. Dolly dedicated her song about strong women, "She's an Eagle When She Flies," to the First Lady.

Reba follows "My Broken Heart" in its climb to the top of *Billboard*'s Hot Country charts.

Naomi and Wynonna Judd provided the most emotionally affecting moment of the evening. Upon receiving the CMA Award for "Best Vocal Duo of the Year," Naomi, who had announced she was quitting the music business because of a chronic, life-threatening liver disease, gave her farewell speech. After she had finished thanking the fans and her pals in Nashville, the audience applauded for several minutes. Reba, now in a sexy lace dress, reappeared to announce the next presenters, but was overtaken by tears and had to stop to catch her breath and regain her composure.

Though nominated for several awards, McEntire didn't win one. But she was happy just to be there, alive, well, and prospering. For the number she performed that evening Reba, clad in a white, jeweled jacket and a huge, floor-length hoop skirt, sang "For My Broken Heart," then called her "good buddy," President Bush ("I can call you that, can't I?" she asked after the fact, to which she received a resounding "Yes!") to the stage. Both George and Barbara planted several kisses on Reba, then the President gave a touching speech on the importance of country music in the lives of all Americans. It was another triumphant appearance for Reba.

Reba performs the National Anthem, her favorite song, at the Country Stars softball game, September 1991.

In November Reba starred in the sequel to the highly rated TV movie *Gambler*, featuring three-time Grammy winner and crossover superstar Kenny Rogers. Offered the part only a few months after the fateful plane crash, a depressed Reba had accepted without even reading the script. "I just wanted to keep busy, and I've always loved those *Gambler* movies—and Kenny, of course." During the filming she kept up a breakneck schedule that allowed her no time for reflection. Flying back and forth between Nashville and Hollywood, Reba was often out of bed by 3 A.M. and returning home twenty-four hours later.

Rogers, who reprised his wildly popular role as

© Carol T. Powers/The White House

Hostess Reba McEntire welcomes "her good buddies," President and Mrs. Bush to the Country Music Association Awards at the Grand Ole Opry in October 1991. It's the first time a President has ever attended.

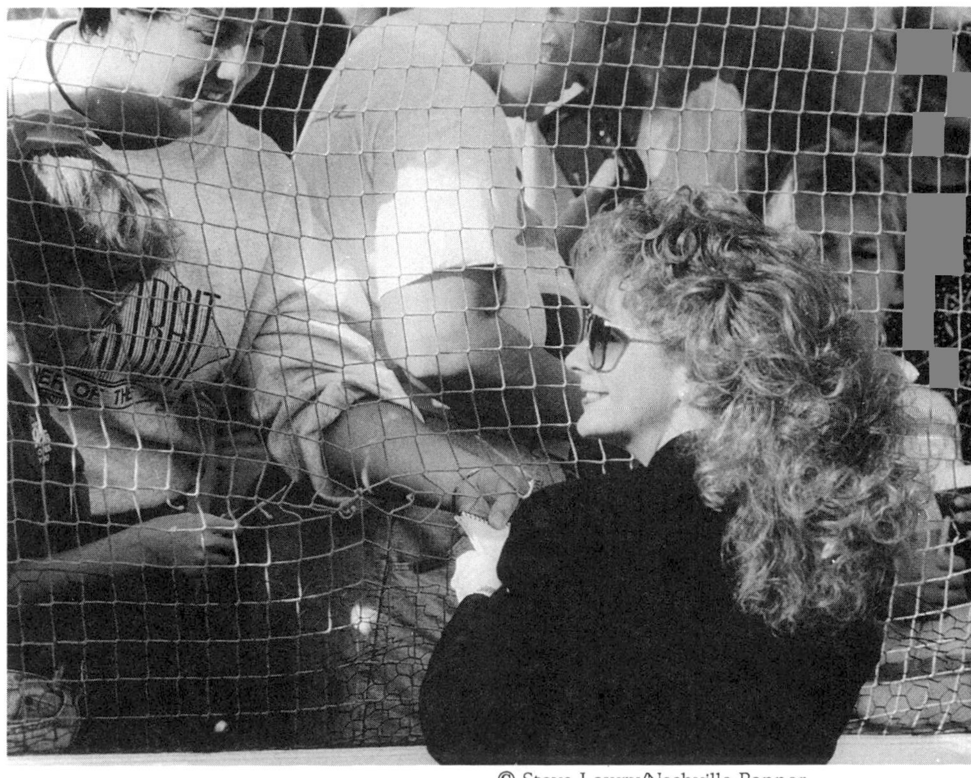

© Steve Lowry/Nashville Banner

Signing autographs for eager fans at the Country Music Association's Country Stars softball game.

Brady Hawkes in *The Gambler*, had seen Reba in *Tremors* and was looking for an "assertive woman with bright red hair" to play former Madame Burgundy Jones. Luckily for everyone, Reba fit the bill.

Broadcast in November on NBC, *The Luck of the Draw* was produced by Ken Kragen and directed by Dick Lowry (who had directed the three previous *Gambler* movies). As Madame Burgundy Jones, Reba played a strong, fiercely determined woman who did whatever she had to in order to save an orphanage. "She's action-packed, and a survivor, just like me," said Reba, who got to ride a horse, shoot a rifle, and look both tough in black leather and seductively feminine in low-cut frocks.

Luck of the Draw featured guest appearances by a slew of former stars of TV westerns: Gene Barry ("Bat Masterson"), James Drury ("The Virginian"), Linda Evans ("Big Valley"—Reba's favorite), Brian Keith ("The Westerner"), Hugh O'Brien ("Wyatt Earp"), Doug McLure ("The Virginian"), Clint Walker ("Cheyenne"), Chuck Connors and Johnny Crawford ("The Rifleman"), Jack Kelly ("Maverick"), Claude Akins ("How the West Was Won"). Also appearing were Patrick McNee ("The Avengers") and David Carradine ("Kung Fu"). Mickey Rooney appeared as a silent film director.

Kenny Rogers found working with Reba a pleasant experience. "For the first three or four weeks on a film set, most people have a decent attitude. And then the romance wears off and they act differently," he said. "Reba never did. She was exactly the same the first day as the last. I applaud her decision to go back to work after the tragedy."

"Working on *The Gambler* was a great experience for me, and a bunch of fun," said Reba. "I really enjoyed doing this movie, and felt like it

There's nothing like a hunky cowboy star to help your acting! Reba with Rick Rossovich, emoting for *The Gambler.*

She can ride, she can shoot, she can keep up with the big boys! Reba as Burgundy Jones, ex-madam, filming *The Gambler.* Left to right: Kenny Rogers, Reba, costar Rick Rossovich.

© Robert Matheu/Retna Ltd.

Miss Reba as Burgundy Jones, the fallen woman with a heart of gold, hams it up on *The Gambler* set.

© Kevin Winter/DMI

Reba McEntire with costar Kenny Rogers on the set of *The Gambler: Luck of the Draw.*

came naturally." Now, even those in the TV audience who might not have known who Reba McEntire was (though that hardly seems possible!) could be numbered among her fans. It seems likely that McEntire will have a healthy acting career if she wants it—nothing is really out of reach for someone with so much determination and talent.

Toward the end of 1991, Reba went to Chicago for an appearance on "The Oprah Winfrey Show." A fashionable but sedate-looking Reba, wearing black stretch pants, an Indian-patterned sweater, and knee-high black boots, talked about her life over the last year. The audience, filled with adoring fans, was solidly there for her. Reba spoke about how her marriage to Narvel had been strengthened by going through pain together, and on a lighter side, when asked if she was going to have any more children, replied, "No, not if Shelby doesn't start behaving better!"

McEntire also told of a letter she'd received that had cheered her considerably. A young girl was roused from a coma while listening to one of Reba's records, and had totally recovered. At the end of the show, Reba conceded that *For My Broken Heart* was the saddest album she'd ever recorded, but said she was trying hard to get on with her life and fulfill all her dreams, since God had given her a second chance, "whatever his reasons."

Applauded as "Outstanding Performer" by *Playboy*, famous enough to be a one-word crossword puzzle clue, and versatile enough to play an elf on the annual "Bob Hope Christmas Special" (in 1991, she sent out Christmas cards showing herself in her green suit with Hope), there is no doubt that the girl who "always wanted to be a singing star" has reached the top of her profession. The trip

The 1991 White House presentation of the First Family's Christmas Seals. Left to right: John D. White, president of the American Lung Association; President Bush; and Reba McEntire, who says of her involvement, "I care not only because I want to breathe cleaner air, but because I want my son to grow up in a healthier environment."

Courtesy of the American Lung Association

Singing along with Aretha Franklin, Barbara Bush, John Denver, and a few of Santa's helpers at the White House Christmas celebration.

The legendary Bob Hope and his favorite elf, Reba McEntire, plug his 1991 Christmas special at the Opryland Hotel.

© Steve Lowry/Nashville Banner

from Oklahoma cowgirl to international superstar has not been without its difficult moments, but Reba McEntire is a superlative example of what can be accomplished with guts, determination, brains, and lots and lots of talent.

Reba McEntire's aim to be the biggest and best never wavers. "I used to say it'd make me happy to record a few hits, but not now. I'm greedy. I want it all," she admits. Sticking with her lifelong philosophy—"Work hard, do the best you can, and good things follow"—Reba's certain everything will work out fine in the end. "I've got trust in the Lord."

Country Music magazine summed up the greatness of Nashville's hardest-working and most popular songstress: "Reba McEntire is the current embodiment of country music's hope for its own future. She is one of the shiniest success stories. Everything she touches seems to turn to gold."

DISCOGRAPHY

Reba McEntire

1978, Mercury
Producer/Jerry Kennedy

Glad I Waited Just for You
One to One
Angel in Your Arms
I Don't Want to Be a One Night Stand
I've Waited All My Life for You
I Was Glad to Give My Everything to You
Take Your Love Away
Between a Woman and a Man
Why Can't He Be You
Invitation to the Blues
Right Time of the Night

Out of a Dream

1979, Mercury
Producer/Jerry Kennedy

Now and Then
Daddy
Last Night Every Night
Makes Me Feel Like a Woman Wants to Feel
That Makes Two of Us
Sweet Dreams
I'm a Woman
Rain Fallin'
Runaway Heart
It's Gotta Be Love

Feel the Fire

1980, Mercury
Producer/Jerry Kennedy

(You Lift Me) Up to Heaven
Tears on My Pillow
I Don't Think Love Ought to Be That Way
Long Distance Lover
If I Had My Way
I Can See Forever in Your Eyes
A Poor Man's Roses (or a Rich Man's Gold)
My Turn
Look at the One (Who's Been Lookin' at You)
Suddenly There's a Valley

Heart to Heart

1981, Mercury
Producer/Jerry Kennedy

Incredibly Blue
Ease the Fever
There Ain't No Love
How Does It Feel to Be Free
Only You (and You Alone)
Today All Over Again
Gonna Love You 'Til the Cows Come Home
Who?
Small Two-Bedroom Starter
Love by Love

Unlimited

1982, Mercury/Polygram
Producer/Jerry Kennedy

I'd Say You
Everything I'll Ever Own
What Do You Know About Heartache
Out of the Blue
Over, Under and Around
I'm Not That Lonely Yet
Whoever's Watchin'
Old Man River (I've Come to Talk Again)
You're the First Time I've Thought About Leaving
Can't Even Get the Blues

Behind the Scene

1983, Mercury/Polygram
Producer/Jerry Kennedy

Love Isn't Love 'Til You Give It Away
Is It Really Love

Reasons
Nickel Dreams
One Good Reason
You Better Love Me After This
There Ain't No Future in This
Why Do We Want What We Know We Can't Have
I Sacrificed More Than You'll Ever Lose
Pins and Needles

Just a Little Love

1984, MCA
Producer/Norro Wilson

Just a Little Love
Poison Sugar
I'm Gettin' Over You
You Are Always There for Me
Every Second Someone Breaks a Heart
Tell Me What's So Good About Goodbye
He Broke Your Memory Last Night
If Only
Congratulations
Silver Eagle

My Kind of Country

1984, MCA
Producer/Harold Shedd

How Blue
That's What He Said
I Want to Hear It from You
It's Not Over (If I'm Not Over You)
Somebody Should Leave
Everything but My Heart
Don't You Believe Him
Before I Met You
He's Only Everything
You've Got Me (Right Where You Want Me)

Have I Got a Deal for You

1985, MCA
Producers/Jimmy Bowen, Reba McEntire

I'm in Love All Over Again
She's Single Again
The Great Divide
Have I Got a Deal for You
Red Roses (Won't Work Now)
Only in My Mind
She's the One Loving You Now
Whose Heartache Is This Anyway?
I Don't Need Nothin' You Ain't Got
Don't Forget Your Way Home

Whoever's in New England

1986, MCA
(gold record)
Producers/Jimmy Bowen, Reba McEntire

Can't Stop Now
You Can Take the Wings Off Me
Whoever's in New England
I'll Believe It When I Feel It
I've Seen Better Days
Little Rock
If You Only Knew
One Thin Dime
Don't Touch Me There
Don't Make That Same Mistake Again

What Am I Gonna Do About You?

1986, MCA (gold record)
Producers/Jimmy Bowen, Reba McEntire

Why Not Tonight
What Am I Gonna Do About You
Lookin' for a New Love Story
Take Me Back
My Mind Is on You
Let the Music Lift You
I Heard Her Cryin'
No Such Thing
One Promise Too Late
'Til It Snows in Mexico

The Last One to Know

1987, MCA (gold record)
Producers/Jimmy Bowen, Reba McEntire

The Last One to Know
The Girl Who Has Everything
Just Across the Rio Grande
I Don't Want to Mention Any Names
Someone Else
What You Gonna Do About Me
I Don't Want to Be Alone
The Stairs
Love Will Find Its Way to You
I've Still Got the Love We Made

Reba McEntire's Greatest Hits

1987, MCA (platinum record)

Just a Little Love
He Broke Your Memory Last Night
How Blue
Somebody Should Leave
Have I Got a Deal for You

Only in My Mind
Whoever's in New England
Little Rock
What Am I Gonna Do About You
One Promise Too Late

Merry Christmas to You

1987, MCA
Producers/Jimmy Bowen, Reba McEntire

Away in a Manger
On This Day
O Holy Night
The Christmas Guest
Silent Night
Happy Birthday Jesus
White Christmas
I'll Be Home for Christmas
A Christmas Letter
Chestnuts Roasting on an Open Fire

Reba

1988, MCA (gold record)
Producers/Jimmy Bowen, Reba McEntire

So, So, So Long
Sunday Kind of Love
New Fool at an Old Game
You're the One I Dream About
Silly Me
Respect
Do Right by Me
I Know How He Feels
Wish I Were Only Lonely
Everytime You Touch Her

Sweet Sixteen

1989, MCA (gold record)
Producers/Jimmy Bowen, Reba McEntire

Cathy's Clown
'Til Love Comes Again
It Always Rains on Saturday
Am I the Only One Who Cares
Somebody Up There Likes Me
You Must Really Love Me
Say the Word
Little Girl
Walk On
A New Love

Reba Live!

1989, MCA (gold record)
Producers/Jimmy Bowen, Reba McEntire

So, So, So Long
One Promise Too Late
Let the Music Lift You Up
Little Rock
New Fool at an Old Game
Little Girl
Can't Stop Now
Sunday Kind of Love
I Know How He Feels
Whoever's in New England
Cathy's Clown
You Must Really Love Me
Somebody Up There Likes Me
San Antonio Rose
Mama Tried
Night Life
Jolene
Sweet Dreams
Respect

Rumor Has It

1990, MCA (gold record)
Producers/Tony Brown, Reba McEntire

Climb That Mountain High
Rumor Has It
Waitin' for the Deal to Go Down
You Lie
Now You Tell Me
Fancy
Fallin' Out of Love
This Picture
You Remember Me
That's All She Wrote

For My Broken Heart

1991, MCA
Producers/Tony Brown, Reba McEntire

For My Broken Heart
Is There Life Out There
Bobby
He's in Dallas
All Dressed Up (with Nowhere to Go)
The Night the Lights Went Out in Georgia
Buying Her Roses
The Greatest Man I Never Knew
I Wouldn't Go That Far
If I Had Only Known

AWARDS

1984

Country Music Association "Female Vocalist of the Year"

1985

Country Music Association "Female Vocalist of the Year"
Academy of Country Music "Top Female Vocalist of the Year"
Music City News "Female Artist of the Year"
Rolling Stone Critics Choice Poll: Top Five Country Artists

1986

Country Music Association "Entertainer of the Year"
Country Music Association "Female Vocalist of the Year"
Academy of Country Music "Top Female Vocalist of the Year"
Music City News "Female Artist of the Year"

1987

Grammy "Best Country Vocal Performance, Female"
American Music Awards "Favorite Country Female Video Artist"
NARM "Best Selling Country Album by a Female Artist"
Academy of Country Music "Top Female Vocalist"
Academy of Country Music "Video of the Year"
Music City News "Female Artist of the Year"
Music City News "Country Music Video of the Year"
Country Music Association "Female Vocalist of the Year"

1988

American Music Awards "Favorite Female Country Vocalist"
Academy of Country Music "Top Female Vocalist"
Music City News "Female Artist of the Year"
TNN Viewers' Choice Awards "Favorite Female Vocalist"
Gallup Youth Survey "Top Ten Female Vocalists"
People Magazine Poll "Top Three Female Vocalists"

1989

American Music Awards "Favorite Female Country Vocalist"
TNN Viewers' Choice Awards "Favorite Female Vocalist"
Music City News "Female Artist of the Year"

1990

American Music Awards "Favorite Female Country Vocalist"

INDEX